D1582234

Bromley Libraries

30128 80293 545 5

THE
CLASSIC *f*M
MUSICAL
TREASURY

THE
CLASSIC *f*M
MUSICAL
TREASURY

A curious collection
of new meanings
for old words

TIM LIHOREAU

First published 2017 by
Elliott and Thompson Limited
27 John Street
London WC1N 2BX
www.eandtbooks.com

ISBN: 978-1-78396-256-3

Copyright © Tim Lihoreau 2017

The Author has asserted his right under the Copyright, Designs and
Patents Act, 1988, to be identified as Author of this Work.

All rights reserved. No part of this publication may be reproduced,
stored in or introduced into a retrieval system, or transmitted, in any
form, or by any means (electronic, mechanical, photocopying, recording or otherwise) without the prior written permission of the publisher.
Any person who does any unauthorized act in relation to this publication may be liable to criminal prosecution and civil claims for damages.

9 8 7 6 5 4 3 2 1

A catalogue record for this book is available from the British Library.

Printed in the UK by TJ International Ltd.

'Words

A letter and a letter on a string
Will hold forever humanity spellbound

Words
Possession of the beggar and the king . . .
Created by man, implicated by mankind

Words
Obsession of the genius and the fool . . .
Read them
Love them'

Words by Anders Edenroth,
The Real Group

CONTENTS

INTRODUCTION

Sometimes I sit and consider the great musical questions of life.

Which came first, Saint-Saens' 'Chickens and Roosters' or Beethoven's 'Egmont'?

Why are we *hear*?

And the big one: is there a conductor?

I have come to the conclusion that while I may never be able to resolve such lofty imponderables, I can at least make a dent in the less crucial issues. Sweat the small stuff, as they say.

Presenting Classic FM's More Music Breakfast is a delight – the privilege of waking the nation every morning with the greatest music this side of the seventeenth century is not lost on me. I love it.

Day in and day out, one thing that never ceases to amaze is the creativity that manifests itself from all around the UK, as ideas are tweeted and one-liners texted to me, emanating from every corner of the country, even before the first soldier of buttered toast has hit the yolk or the first shot of espresso can send its dopamine blast into the prefrontal cortex.

Indeed, so nooked and crannied is this green and pleasant land that many places have necessitated a gander through the atlas to educate myself about exactly where each listener is listening. It was in an effort to both unite and thank our listeners from these disparate places that we came up with the idea for this book.

The Classic FM Musical Treasury is an attempt to write a new – and not entirely serious (one might even say entirely fictitious) – musical language for our age; to document those many musical and arts-based terms, concepts and objects that you may well have experienced or heard of but for which, until now, there was no name. What better way to do it than by paying tribute to the towns and villages, the suburbs, hamlets, digs, dens, the quarters and quoins of this beautiful land of ours?

Many listeners sent me the names of their favourite places: their home towns and beloved haunts. Classic FM presenters, too, suggested their favourite locations and many have been incorporated into the *Treasury*.

Modestly, I would like to say that the offering within is nothing short of a new music bible. Where Groves has no word for, say, a particularly

poisonous music critic, the *Treasury* will step in
(see page 201). When you need to know the name
for that person who always sees fit to clap in the
golden silence at the end of an amazing live performance, it's here (page 137).

Have you ever wondered what the correct term
is for that free CD that came with a newspaper and
has been hanging around in your car for months doing double duty as an ice scraper during the winter
months? Wonder no longer (page 145). And why not
enlighten yourself should you come across a *bimbister*
(page 161); be forewarned before encountering a
particularly stroppy *carlton in lindrick* (page 62); and
feel a tad superior that you could, in an emergency,
quickly locate a musician's *poole keynes* (page 98).
Quite a talent.

Geographically speaking, we have traversed
the United Kingdom. From Grumbla to Inverkip,
Thrushelton to Roundthwaite; from Ballogie to
Cofton Hackett, and Aberargie to Wetley Rocks, the
Treasury covers it all, offering definitions for music
lovers, instrumentalists, choir singers, enthusiasts
and professionals alike. No musical stone is left un-
turned, and I hope you enjoy it.

How to use this book

Suggestion one: chapters have been organised the-matically to enable you to explore areas of particular musical interest, such as festivals, choral singing, opera and dance, or composers and their composi-tions. Use the index to explore the words that are cross-referenced in those definitions to find further new terms.

Suggestion two: just read it.

Tim Lihoreau,
February 2017

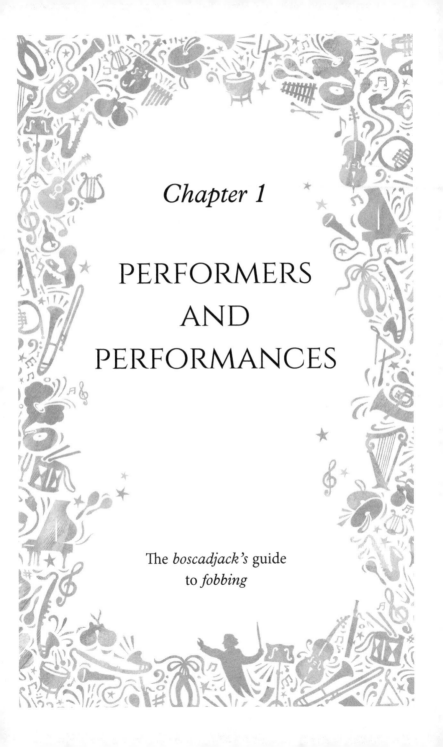

Chapter 1

PERFORMERS
AND
PERFORMANCES

The *boscadjack's* guide
to *fobbing*

burniestrype *(n.)*

standard programme notes used verbatim by lazy promoters to fill their expensive souvenir programmes, usually lifted from the internet without attribution.

billinge *(n.)*

formal term for a 'musicals' singer's programme biog. Popularly believed to be so-named because it is obligatory to contain a reference to a performer having appeared in *The Bill*. This is not true. It is, however, an Equity requirement that appearances in *Casualty* must be itemised.

forgue *(n.; slang)*

a concert that attracts older people. Similar to the description of, say, Worthing as 'the eternal waiting room', *forgue* is thought to have originated as a portmanteau combination of an old English fair and a morgue.

clifton campville *(n.)*

a musical variety act involving the use of a puppet or person-sized cuddly toy.

kirkibost *(n.)*

a concert in a small country church by a local group

that charges central Mayfair prices for its tickets both to raise maximum money for the already pristine church's refurbishment appeal and because its parishioners all live and work in central Mayfair from Sunday night to Saturday anyway.

cat bank *(n.; slang)*
names in a fixer's little black book that can be called on when a diva falls ill.

hilliard's cross *(n.)*
the throwing of one's toys out of the pram in rehearsal over a first-world issue (such as a perceived lack of decent macchiato), expressed in an unsuitably high-pitched voice.

balnaknock *(n.; pron. bal-na-NOK)*
the sound made when a conductor taps his baton on his music stand to signal to the orchestra that he is about to begin.

cnoc ard *(n.)*
a particularly resonant *balnaknock* (q.v.) used either on the first morning of the season or to express annoyance.

chatto *(n.)*
the pre-rehearsal hubbub generated by an orchestra, prior to the *balnaknock* (q.v.).

wallsuches *(n.; German; pron. VAL-zukkers)*
dry asides made by a conductor in rehearsal often followed by a large sniff, meriting a mannered titter from the assembled musicians or singers.

kinknockie *(n.; pron. KINK-nokki)*
a pastime which the visiting conductor is rumoured to be into but about which no one has the slightest clue.

fobbing *(v.)*
'marking', or not fully singing, a part in rehearsal specifically for dubious reasons, such as saving one's voice, the humidity of the room or the bad karma of the ley lines.

tosside *(n.)*
the dubious practice of not speaking in between concerts in order to protect one's voice. Also known as *stoke bliss*.

kirivick *(n.)*
any of the various teas, balms and sweets that singers swear by for maintaining their voices but that appear to everyone else to be naught but snake oil.

market drayton *(n.)*
a rehearsal pencil magnetically attached to the music stand.

market overton *(n.)*
a rehearsal pencil, sharpened to half-length, and stored behind the ear.

bassingbourn-cum-kneesworth *(n.)*
position of legs adopted by orchestral musicians in rehearsal, one foot placed on knee of other leg, when they are in a long period of bars' rest.

partrishow *(n.)*
the curious period prior to a concert when members of the orchestra (who are shortly to elevate you onto a musical plane with their amazing playing, somewhere between channelling divinity and manifesting rapture) potter onto the stage in ones and twos, handbags and occasionally knitting in

tow before proceeding to settle their cardigans on their seats, play warm-up doodles and blow spittle through their instruments.

chance's pitch *(n.)*
being already in tune when given the oboist's A.

aish *(n.)*
the note used to tune the orchestra at the New Year's Day concert, the morning after the New Year's Eve party.

whiteflat *(n.)*
a bum note or tuning issue that is only audible to musicians and leaves others wondering what the problem is.

fintry *(n.)*
the area just outside the entrance to the stage, where the conductor/soloist pauses to say 'toi toi toi' before going on.

ashow *(n.; pron. AY-show)*
the traditional piece of modern music that has been performed just before the entry of the conductor

at every orchestral concert since time immemorial. Usage example, overheard at interval at Philharmonic Hall, Liverpool: 'Sorry I was late. Boss asked for Monday's figures today. Missed the *ashow*, but slipped in just as they started the first movement.'

kyles stockinish *(adj.)*
descriptive of a twenty-first-century orchestra that performs while dressed as their nineteenth-century equivalents, in full ball gowns and breeches, their gritted smiles masking venomous looks at their leader for making them undergo this form of modern-day torture.

logie pert *(n.)*
a group of fake stage musicians, dressed in black, all of whom are schooled in looking beautiful and bowing in the same direction. Not to be confused with *new invention* (q.v.).

nant-fforch *(n.)*
a form of 'orchestra' increasingly common in musicals that appears to feature only one player on each instrument, and a conductor with one hand on the piano.

flappit spring *(n.)*

a particularly energetic page turner who detracts from the performance by shooting up from their chair and turning the page in the style of someone spanking a child.

bargod *(n.)*

person with immaculate sense of rhythm who will give colleagues the nod if they want to read a book in long rest passages. Orchestral equivalent of the 'designated driver'.

wotter *(n.; slang)*

a veteran member of an orchestra whom the music committee have been trying to oust for years because they object to everything *and* look bad on TV.

shootash *(n.)*

the strange synchronicity that enables a musician to sneeze only in their bars of rest – and, perhaps more intriguingly, in time to the music.

barshare *(v.)*

sarcastic term for when an orchestral player fails to come in. Usage example, Klemperer: 'Oboe, where were you at F? (Pause.) Or did you think you were *barsharing* with the flutes and this is not your morning?' See also *wallsuches*.

askham richard *(n.; pron. ASKam riKARD)*
bridge rules used by brass players during multi-bar rests. Named after the originator, Richard Strauss, who developed the rules as a bastardisation of his favourite card game, skat.

barripper *(n.)*
passage the trombones have played for years, often in their *Orchestral Excerpts* book, and enjoy playing so much that, when it pops up in a concert performance, they shred the ears of the back desks of the cello section.

prees *(n.)*
the pre-performance rituals of a piano soloist, which traditionally include altering the height of the piano stool, the flapping of garments, and a seemingly eternal period of head-down reflection, prior to looking up at the conductor to indicate readiness.

glenbervie *(n.)*
a small noise emitted in anguish by a pianist while playing, as perfected by Glenn Gould and Keith Jarrett.

sonning eye *(n.)*
the condition of the eyeball rolling upwards under the eyelid, in the manner of a pianist enjoying an ecstatic moment of their own playing.

alum rock *(n.)*
the emphatic (and some might say affected) nod of the head performed by a pianist who has just played a significant or poignant full-hands chord on their instrument, as if the chord somehow had a ripple effect in time and space.

fladdibister *(v.)*
the action of an accompanist whose soloist has inadvertently cut a section of music in performance, leaving them to *fladdibister* until they can work out where the soloist has cut to.

middle brighty *(n.)*
the temporary confidence of a concerto soloist after

the tough opening section but before the fiendish ending.

cowbit *(n.)*
the final high note of an aria, just after the long trill and before the orchestra's rush to the end, tradition-ally snatched at by an irascible diva.

warblington *(n.)*
a singer in musicals whose motto seems to be: 'If in doubt, vibrato.'

kirtling *(n.)*
the aural assault experienced when a singer keeps the same word of a song going while following a flor-id tune, which appears to have been written using a very wobbly pen.

higham gobion *(n.; archaic)*
a coloratura soprano. The term is thought to date from a time when they were considered witch-like, i.e. from the 1970s to the present day.

low friarside *(n.)*
genre of bass singer usually identified by their black

clothes, long white hair and beard, full-length black Barbour coats and black felt hats; one who looks every inch a bass and knows it.

bottisham *(n.)*
the feeling of numbness experienced by the bass soloist who is in only one of the 78 movements of an oratorio but has to sit on stage all the while without shuffling.

lochend *(n.; Scots)*
a new singer on the block with serious delusions of grandeur.

curry mallet *(n.; colloquial)*
a big star who is brought in at great expense and yet with minimal benefit. Usage example, overheard at Colston Hall, Bristol, in the green room: 'I'm not sure where they found this soloist, but he's balls-ing it up royally. About as much use as a *curry mallet.*'

boscadjack *(n.; old Cornish)*
the latest tenor on the block. Usage example, *Scotsman* concert review, August 2011: 'Last night's

closing gala concert was a mixed bag. The orchestra was on fine form, as was our esteemed soloist who gave a plucky rendition of the Bruch. However, the evening was marred when a smirking, chiselled *boscadjack* started the second half by schlepping out a few film themes and Neapolitan numbers. If I'd had pizza in my pocket, I would have thrown it at him.'

auchertool *(n.)*
soloist who overplays his Scottish roots to the extent that he is prepared to wear a fictitious brand of tartan kilt when singing either north of the border or on daytime TV shows.

asserby turn *(n.)*
the movement of a full-figured soprano soloist who, having taken appreciative applause from her audience, attempts to weave through the violin section to the stage exit, sending violin parts wafting from stands as she goes.

cotton of brighty *(n.)*
a show-stealing dress, sometimes of a patriotic nature though not exclusively so, designed to attract

attention and worn by female soloists and Jean-Yves Thibaudet. See also *backmuir of new gilston*.

backmuir of new gilston *(n.)*
the situation that occurs when one eye-catching outfit (see *cotton of brighty*) is not enough to steal a show. During a *backmuir of new gilston*, the soloist gives the impression that there is an endless *cotton of brighty* selection backstage and that she intends to wear each one before the end of the night.

darcy lever *(n.)*
the moment in a musical when the director has insisted his attractive male star sheds some clothes for purely artistic reasons.

acton beauchamp *(n.)*
an actor who cannot sing.

singleborough *(n.)*
a singer who cannot act.

chinnor *(n.)*
the unsettling expression – mouth extended low, steely eyes – adopted by singers wanting to show menace.

kemsing *(v.)*

to sing and look vaguely tragic at the same time, a technique beloved of most tenors, particularly Placido Domingo.

spreakley *(n.)*

the part of a song where the singer speaks over the instrumental accompaniment in a strangely contorted way; often used to reveal that the singer is only dreaming or, in the case of the audience, having a nightmare.

dauntsey lock *(n.)*

the pose adopted by a singer in a musical when belting out a showstopper, involving both arms raised at 25 degrees above horizontal and a smile permanently fixed to full beam.

lower stanton st quintin *(n.)*

formal name for the classic stance often performed towards the end of a song in a musical, where the legs are planted firmly apart while the arms rise slowly upwards, inviting triumphant applause regardless of quality.

crymych arms *(n.)*

the first position learned by recital singers. Refers to the adoption of the unnatural 'down and round, hands cupped' stance, as if clutching an invisible medicine ball to the abdomen.

edradynate *(n.)*

the occasional mist or spray emitted by singers.

haugh *(v.)*

to extend the mouth in rectangular fashion, an action often forced on a singer when reaching for high notes, with eyeballs rolling into the upper eyelids.

eype's mouth *(n.)*

the shape of a singer's lips when trying to mask the challenge of reaching the note with what she thinks is a smile; the reality is perhaps closer to The Joker from *Batman*.

cathole *(n.; archaic)*

the mouth of a female singer, thought to have originated in the theatre. Usage example, from the original draft of *A Midsummer Night's Dream*: DEMETRIUS – 'O Helena, goddess, nymph, perfect, divine, / To what, my love, shall I compare thine eyne? / Crystal is muddly. Oh, how ripe in show, / Thy cathole, those kissing cherries, tempting grow.'

corpusty *(n.)*
a perfectly pleasant vocal rendition that is lacking a certain something more to bring it to life.

ellerdine *(adj.)*
improvisational and generally pleasant-sounding, in the manner of Ella Fitzgerald's scat singing.

zoar *(v.)*
to coin a new word or noise while scat singing that doesn't really work because it sounds comical or reminiscent of another word. Usage example, overheard at Ronnie Scott's: 'He was amazing. Never heard a trio like that before. (Pause.) Could do without the singer, though. Was she just *zoaring* or did she keep going on about spuds?'

troon *(v.)*
to sing along to a piece of music, doo-be-dooing pleasantly, in the style of a Swingle Singer.

earby *(n.)*

someone who places a finger in one ear while singing and raising their eyes heavenwards. Very occasionally, this is to enable them to hear their inner note but more often it's because they saw the Swingle Singers do it on *The Two Ronnies* back in the 1970s. See also *folkestone*.

folkestone *(n.; archaic)*

an old English word for the person who puts a finger in one ear, sings of a blond-haired maiden and adopts a Cornish accent, despite hailing from Dudley. Similar but different from an *earby* (q.v.).

kennegy *(adj.)*

descriptive of a performer with an innate air of the maverick about them, making you feel that anything might happen.

dings, the *(n.)*

technical term for the ten-, five- and two-minute bells in the interval of a concert.

barend *(n.)*

1. the point at which the shutter is loudly brought

down on the drinks counter in a small concert hall, midway through the second half, thus shattering the poignant sections of a rather lovely concerto.

2. *(slang)* the combination of one thin and one thick line at the end of a piece of sheet music.

pleasington *(n.)*

a short piece of orchestral music, verging on a lollipop, that is universally known and loved, which is placed in the second half of a concert in order that everyone sits through the godawful modern piece without leaving.

happisburgh *(n.; pron. HAZEburgh)*

the one movement of a suite or set of variations that everybody knows and loves and that makes it all worthwhile. See, conversely, *basta*.

coffinswell *(n.)*

the moment in a performance when the seasonal coughs reach their climax, forcing the conductor to turn round and deliver a hard stare.

sutton montis *(n.)*

the rare moment in a concert where the conductor

will stop proceedings to turn to the audience, berate and in some instances publicly shame the person whose phone just beeped loudly during the slow movement.

hadlow stair *(n.)*
a complex manoeuvre experienced only rarely in a live concert and that can be performed only by the world's greatest conductors. It involves a contorted turn of the head towards the audience, while still conducting, and a gorgon-like gaze at the one person who forgot to turn their stupid phone off (or similar). See also *jacks hatch* and *sutton montis*.

thrushelton *(n.)*
a conductor's manic lunge, which spatters beads of sweat onto the first desk of the strings and is designed to (a) get the orchestra to play more loudly and (b) make the conductor look great on TV.

largoward *(n.)*
the treacly mush that can occur when a conductor, despite his violent mannerisms, can't stop the orchestra from slowing down and what was once a *maestoso* becomes a *largo con slowmo*.

offley *(n.)*

a state of discrepancy between two parties from their desired simultaneous beat, existing in many forms.

little offley is common in small venues, outdoor fetes, etc., when soloist and accompanist become separated on their musical journey.

great offley is common at sporting events and more often described as *lagness* (q.v.); arises when the soloist's rendition of the national anthem is at least three beats in front of the terrace's version.

high offley is a particular type witnessed when a soloist and conductor are locked in battle over the correct speed for an aria or concerto and, as such, should be deemed more a spectator sport than a matter of concern.

Finally, *offley rock* is increasingly common. It occurs when pop singers cannot hear their backing tracks, affecting not just time but pitch, and it should not be missed for the world.

flugarth *(n.)*

the manner of conducting where the shapes of two concentric circles are made by the conductor's arms, over and over again, a method of no damn use whatsoever for players.

bootle-cum-linacre *(n.)*
the name Sir Thomas Beecham gave his lucky spats, without which he would not conduct.

breage *(n.; pron. bree-ARJH)*
a measure of bounce, relating to hair, specifically of conductors. Usage example, *i* review, January 2014: 'Sir Simon was on sensational form, although apparently incorporating his gym workout with his conducting style these days. For most of the finale of Beethoven's Ninth, the *breage* was so off-putting, I could hardly see the orchestra.'

camel's head *(n.)*
the 'sex face' adopted by some conductors, delighted with their in-concert efforts.

achalone *(n.)*
a single solitary clap at the end of a movement, deemed to be out of place and usually silenced with a frosty reception from the stage.

basta *(n.)*

the one movement of a favourite suite that no one minds missing out in order to make the concert the right length. See, conversely, *happisburgh*.

flishinghurst *(n.)*

an affected flourish, of either the hand or instrument or bow, enacted by a concerto soloist during a performance to suggest they are divinely channelling the composer's thoughts at that very moment, rather than knocking it out for the third time this month.

east suisnish *(n.)*

conductors' term for a medium flourish of the right hand intended to bring off the double-basses on their final *pp pizzicato* note.

ednol *(n.)*

the flourish of the head used particularly by keyboard players to ensure all players end together. Not to be confused with a *roundthwaite* (q.v.).

roundthwaite *(n.)*

the 'round and up' motion of chamber players, made with the instruments themselves, that signals to fellow players that they should all stop playing simultaneously. Not to be confused with an *ednol* (q.v.). Usage example, overheard at Sage Gateshead foyer music rehearsal: 'Sebastian, I'll follow you at the coda, so we don't balls it up, then we'll all look at Jemima for the *roundthwaite*. Yes?'

arncroach *(v.)*
to stagger in a faux-unruly way while singing 'Rule, Britannia' at the end of a gala concert, sober all the while, but thus invading your neighbour's space to the tune of one Union flag up the nose.

istead rise *(n.)*
the taking of the last line of a song, often a national anthem, into a higher register for its conclusion, regardless of the musical appeal of so doing. Chiefly performed at sporting events, often by *cleghorns* (q.v.), simply to prove it can be done.

allington bar *(n.)*
1. dreaded by amateur conductors, the moment near the end of a piece, in the middle of the race to the finish line, in which all forces are suddenly back together again, playing and/or singing. Out of all the bars in

the work, the *allington bar* has the maximum potential for disaster. Or, from an audience's perspective,

2. the delicious moment towards the end of a piece of music where the full orchestra comes together, resulting in a tingle down the spine.

dorney reach *(n.)*
the traditional shaking of hands between conductor and the leader of the orchestra post-performance.

craven arms *(n.)*
the surreal 'arm tennis' that is occasionally exchanged in the ecstasy of post-performance between soloist and conductor (and occasionally the orchestra) in the middle of a stage, set to tumultuous applause and involving pointing the arms sideways: 'It was all you!'; 'No, it was all you!'

st blazey gate *(n.)*
the triumphant walk performed by conductor and/or soloist from offstage to centre front to receive rapturous applause. See also *grunasound*.

grunasound *(n.)*
a misjudged *st blazey gate* (q.v.) that has left the

soloist or conductor walking out onto the stage to receive applause that is already dying down. A noble audience will dig deep and find more to give, avoiding the embarrassment that otherwise awaits the soloist rising from a bow only to be greeted by streams of audience members, rucksacks on backs, rushing to catch last orders and the last train to Croydon.

withiel florey *(n.)*
a small child in unfeasibly smart clothes, usually related to one of the backstage staff, who is sent out to give a bouquet to an artist at the end of a concert.

combebow *(n.)*
a standard stage bow, which involves a full bend and staying down for the length of time it takes to say 'thank you very much' under the breath, before standing up.

fanshawe *(n.)*
the return to the stage to receive applause at the end of a concert, a journey that must be undertaken only in the certainty of sufficiently strong applause to cover your walk back. See also *forncett end*.

enmore *(n.)*

the glance exchanged offstage between conductor and soloist, when deciding whether to risk going back for another *fanshawe* (q.v.).

forncett end *(n.)*

the state of affairs when a *fanshawe* (q.v.) has been incorrectly judged, resulting in a silent, nervous shuffle off the stage at the same time as the orchestra.

bargate *(n.)*

the inquest in the pub after the concert to find out which bloody musician actually came in early, wrecking a beautiful moment.

shatterling *(n.)*

a venomous, snide comment on someone's performance, concealed within a seemingly platitudinous pleasantry. Usually delivered in a pub after a concert or at the first rehearsal the morning after. For example: 'I really enjoyed the first night of the Messiaen, last night.' 'Oh, thank you.' 'Yes, how brave of you to throw away the rule book *and* the composer's manuscript too!'

darkland *(n.)*

the late-night post-gig period when, having returned home from a performance, a musician feels unable to go straight to bed, so wanders around a dimly lit house, family asleep, making a sandwich or flaking out in front of *Storage Hunters*.

daywall *(n.)*

the point reached, on a musician's day off work, when the sheen of delight in not having to work begins to pall.

muscoate *(n.; pron. MUSE-coat)*

a second job taken on by a musician in order to maintain a basic standard of living when the muse herself sees fit not to provide it. Usage example, overheard in Imperial College bar, late one evening: 'After this I've got just an Alpine Symphony in September then I'm done. Gonna have to fall back on the *muscoate*. (Pause.) I don't suppose *you* want any plastering done, do you?'

kippilaw *(n.)*

the unwritten rule that says if you work in an orchestra, performing until 11.30 p.m. each night and arriving home in the early hours of the morning, even with an empty house to yourself every day till 4 p.m., you will still never be able to catch up on all the sleep missed.

kippilaw mains *(n.)*
the three sub-tenets of *kippilaw* (q.v), which state that (1) sleep at the wrong time of day doesn't feel like real sleep, (2) when you want to sleep you can't and vice versa, and (3) if you ever have more than fifteen minutes' peace alone in the house, a cold caller *will* ring.

giggety *(adj.)*
descriptive of the appearance of a musician in the throes of a long period of evening engagements, which he daren't turn down for fear of lack of future work but which leads him to be mistaken for a member of the walking dead.

gigg *(n.)*
a much sought-after engagement, sometimes round Christmas time but more often a private party, where the musicians are paid over £2,000.

glen parva *(n.)*
any British conductor who has ever seriously considered changing his name to something more mysterious sounding in the hope of getting more work.

gladestry *(n.)*
the emphatic and ever-so-slightly forced words of congratulations given by a singer on hearing that another has landed a well-paid gig.

cleghorn *(n.)*
person whose credentials for singing the national anthem at a national sporting event include having legs to die for.

kinloid *(adj.)*
descriptive of the family members assuming key roles within a singer's entourage without first having mastered the finer points normally associated with the job, namely: management technique, knowledge of the business, and preventing their own knuckles from dragging along the floor as they walk.

gobowen *(n.)*
a young and bearded proponent of classical music

who makes a good living performing concerts in jeans, T-shirt and trainers while penning articles for the broadsheets about how classical music is out of date and elitist.

brinsop *(n.)*
an album of songs containing the singer's pet favourites, which they are allowed to record from time to time – at a ratio of 1:5 – so long as they keep doing the serious stuff in between.

wormelow tump *(n.)*
a favourite film theme that has had dubious Italian lyrics grafted on to make it suitable for every *boscadjack* (q.v.) to put on their debut (possibly only) album.

blackbird leys *(n.)*
the mid-to-late-career album of Beatles covers issued by an attractive instrumentalist.

charterville allotments *(n.)*
a now illegal arrangement between artists' managers and record companies in which places in the hit parade could be guaranteed for the occasional token classical act.

steeple bumpstead *(n.)*

a particular type of classical singer who, when invited to sing popular music on a TV Christmas special, proceeds to sing Burt Bacharach hits, producing a sound somewhere between Montserrat Caballé and Queen Victoria.

brynhovah *(n.)*

any singer thought to have the potential to 'save' classical music and whose albums are automatically given marketing budgets set at ten times the amount of money they eventually bring in. Not to be confused with a *boscadjack* (q.v.).

blank bank *(n.; slang)*

crossover duo.

charnage *(n.)*

any week when more than four crossover acts dominate the classical music chart's top ten.

wambrook *(n.)*

a piece of music that enters the Classic FM Hall of Fame unexpectedly following a three-month online, email and social media campaign by the composer.

brasted chart *(n.)*

an index of classical music releases rumoured to exist in record company circles; contains the accurate list of sales figures once all albums containing '*Gabriel's Oboe*' have been removed.

cockenzie and port seton *(n.)*

a short-lived piano and vocal duo set up by a record company to rival Flanders and Swann in the late 1950s. Sadly dropped after their debut release, 'She was a smooth operetta, and, by jove, she could go low', failed to chart.

aston juxta mondrum *(n.)*

formal term for any 'classical' singer who ventures onto *Britain's Got Talent*, *The Voice* or *X Factor* in order for the producers to cover all markets.

upstreet *(v.)*

to musically up-cycle by taking a pop song into the choral or orchestral domain while making sure that the feel and spirit of the original are completely lost.

girlsta *(n.)*
precocious prodigy who starts in classical music then transfers to pop.

beausale *(n.)*
a musician whose attractive physical appearance is the very *last* thing on their record company's mind, despite it never having done their chart positions any harm.

naunton beauchamp *(n.)*
the unspoken but widely observed tendency of concert television directors to dwell on the attractive players.

chetnole *(n.)*
a jazz singer with the craggy face of a gunslinger but the soulful voice of an angel.

new invention *(n.)*
a band created by a former Grumbleweed, who saw a gap in the market for a TV-friendly group of classical musicians to play on pop and rock tracks; now the only such name in the little black book of seemingly every TV booker.

lletty harry *(n.)*
Swansea-based Blondie tribute band.

leven seat *(n.)*
the particularly cheesy moment in a boy band's TV performance of their Christmas single when the key abruptly changes up a tone, and each band member steps off his white leatherette stool and walks forwards.

baldhu *(n.)*
member of a classical boy band attempting a come-back ten years later.

four crosses *(n.; slang)*
a truly awful performance by someone who should consider a change of career, thought to be derived from the judges on *Britain's Got Talent*.

fordell *(n.)*
a style of singing that makes the most of the break in the voice, very popular with *X Factor* contestants and retired Swiss singers.

liphook *(n.)*
a male pop/rock star who has both a slight curling of

the upper lip and a seemingly innate power to make people swoon.

drumpellier *(v.)*
to propel oneself from the drummer's platform while performing in a glam rock band. Usage example, from John Bonham's diaries, July 1972: 'Played the Kooyong in Melbourne. Jimmy climbed on my riser and nearly kicked in my Ludwigs. Then *drumpelliered* himself, landing flat on his face. Serves him right. He owes me new sticks. Gig cut short.'

upper dicker *(n.)*
the one person in a rock group of four or more people who never agrees with the rest and is held responsible for the 'artistic differences' and subsequent break-up of the group.

funzie *(n.)*
the glam rock one-piece jump suit, as worn by Freddie Mercury.

aynho *(adj.)*
1. descriptive of the brightly coloured spectacle frames common in 1980s Buggles videos and now

favoured only by visiting Scandinavian soloists.

2. a now-unavailable Ikea bookshelf.

little earnock *(n.)*

a small electronic device used by rock musicians, placed inside the ear to hear one's own output; when malfunctioning, has the capacity to play an entirely different song from the one the rest of the band is playing – with painful auditory results.

bont *(n.)*

the micro-unit of money paid to an artist each time their music is played on Spotify.

booleybank *(n.)*

the online account set up some years ago to channel an artist's Spotify earnings, which can sometimes top several pence.

diglis *(n.)*

record company term for the latest format of audio, short for 'digital listening', and now reinvented every two years in order to persuade people to buy the same music again.

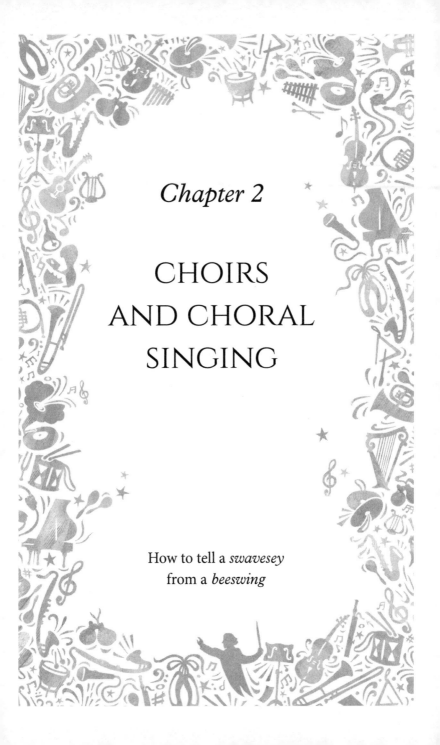

Chapter 2

CHOIRS
AND CHORAL
SINGING

How to tell a *swavesey*
from a *beeswing*

chilton cantelo *(n.)*

the cold temperature at which it is physically impossible for a church choir to sing, adopted as the compulsory nave temperature of all churches by both Vatican II in 1965 and the General Synod in 1970.

colkirk *(n.)*

the grumpy church warden whose job it is, prior to a concert, to keep the temperature to the regulation *chilton cantelo* (q.v.).

warbleton *(n.)*

an unconfident vicar whose sole qualm about seeking holy orders was the fear of having to intone the responses to a choir each week, but who nevertheless gives it their best shot. The modern-day spelling, *warbleton*, is an elision of the original *warble-lieutenant*.

allhallows on sea *(n.)*

any requiem performed by the local church choir.

little boys heat *(n.; slang)*

the fug in the choir practice room of St Paul's Cathedral.

amen corner *(n.)*

the moment, fifteen seconds before the end of Handel's *Messiah*, after the pause but before the final notes, when a hundred people all make anxious eye contact with the conductor.

godalming *(n.)*

a contemporary composer who writes poignant religious choral music, perfect for the montages on *Children in Need*, inspired 'by the beauty of God's earth' as witnessed from the French windows of his desirable Oxfordshire barn. Not to be confused with a *godmersham* (q.v.).

godmersham *(n.)*

a contemporary composer who writes poignant religious choral music yet does not believe in God.

glororum *(n.)*

pleasant, choral, polyphonic Polyfilla; the choral equivalent of *ballogie* works (q.v.). Usage example, overheard at the last London A Cappella Festival: 'Mmm, that was good I have to admit but, well, there are only so many cluster chords I can take. I hope they do *Panis angelicus* or some other such *glororum* in the second half.'

latimer *(n.)*

a piece of choral music whose words have had to be translated into Italian or Latin in order to disguise the fact that they sound truly banal in English.

anchor *(n.; pron. AN-kor)*

any visiting choir, often German, which dazzles audiences with its flawless polyphony, astounding moustaches and Photoshop smiles, allowing the local paper to pull out its 'UNITED IN SONG' headline yet again.

llanfihangel cwmdu *(n.)*

any clichéd, traditional song used since time immemorial to represent how Welsh male-voice choirs are typical of 'the land of song' in much the same way as a Routemaster bus is used in every American film to denote England.

ceann a'choinich *(n.)*

the over-produced sound of a pseudo-Gaelic choir used on pop records since the dawn of Clannad.

four alls, the *(n.; slang)*

choirmasters' term for the morning following the

informal summer concert, i.e. the last day of the year/season; so called because the four 'all's are accomplished: All Souls, Michael and All Angels, All Saints, and all else.

yeldersley hollies *(n.)*
collective noun for the group of Christmas popular songs, rearranged for flawless choral groups, which are deemed acceptable in a classical setting so long as the choir wear Christmas jumpers.

carol green *(n.)*
the Pantone reference for the colour of the original *Carols for Choirs, Book 1*.

tradespark *(n.)*
any sparkly bling added to a choir's standard uniform to make them 'feel a little bit more Christmassy', despite the fact that it makes over 90 per cent of them far more grumpy to wear it.

langlee mains *(n.; pron. lanGLEE MAINS)*
American term for the favoured pose of a barbershop choir, involving the arms stretched wide to about two metres and a fixed beaming smile just slightly wider.

swavesey *(n.)*

the cheesy side-to-side motion, stepping from foot to foot, beloved of barbershop competition choirs.

beeswing *(n.)*

same as a *swavesey* (q.v.) except starting on the off beat.

blarmachfoldach *(n.)*

formal term for the music portfolio for a male-voice choir.

efail isaf *(n.)*

a lollipop in the repertoire of a male-voice choir that is *guaranteed* to please, such as 'Guide Me, O Thou Great Redeemer'.

ventongimps *(n.)*

veteran female choir singers whose range, over the years, has extended further and further downwards, leading them to present themselves as 'Domingos in disguise' to compensate for the universal dearth of available tenors.

ty'n-y-byrwydd *(n.;Welsh)*
counter tenor.

trimstone *(adj.)*
descriptive of a veteran female choral singer whose vibrato has become so pronounced she resembles a 1970s TrimPhone.

catacol *(n.)*
the sound that one shrill vibrato makes when it cuts through an entire choir of pleasant female voices.

kettlesing *(v.)*
to add a glissando vocal effect where it is not called for, achieved by either (a) the soprano section of a choir when a little daunted by the high bit or (b) a millennial singing in the style of their favourite pop star.

kettlesing bottom *(n.)*
the clenched buttocks of one about to *kettlesing* (q.v.).

calfsound *(n.)*
the tones heard when the higher basses in a choir attempt to go low, accompanied by patronising looks

from the sopranos and altos, not to mention smug grins from the *alloway* (q.v.).

foolow *(n.; pron. FOO-lov)*
a bass who insists that he can sing the ridiculous-ly low section of the Russian choral piece despite clearly producing only a breathy, half-strength note resembling someone in an iron lung.

alloway *(n.)*
a bass who can sing *so* low as to cause comment in the soprano and alto sections.

clachan of campsie *(n.)*
the altos' first run-through of their part.

allt-yr-grug *(n.)*
the chuntering noise made by altos when they realise their part is a line of middle Cs again. See also *alt hill*.

alt hill *(adj.)*
descriptive of the often weird leaps of the alto line, leaving the section in no doubt that they are there merely to fill in the harmony. See also *allt-yr-grug*.

keeston *(n.)*
the one person in a choir who hits the note every time and is, therefore, much sought after as an immediate neighbour by others.

keyworth *(n.)*
the chap in the tenor section who always – *always* – points out the bit you got wrong after every concert.

edgeworth *(n.)*
a chorus singer who spends plenty of time ensuring that his page corners are all folded in advance (see *edgebolton*) but not enough time actually learning the music.

badachonacher *(n.)*
the half-syllable of a word sung by a chorus member one beat before they were supposed to.

baddidarroch *(adj.)*
descriptive of the end of a great choral moment, when seemingly every choral singer has come off the last note at a different time.

higher rads end *(n.)*

the lucky moment when you finish on the wrong note in a choral work but it happens to fit the harmony anyway.

fodderstone gap *(n.; pron. FOSTON gap)*

the difference between the key in which an *a cappella* choir starts and the key that, after a quick run to the piano and a resounding of the final chord, proves to be the one it ends in.

keyhaven *(n.)*

the easy section of a piece that is very well known to, and liked by, the choir, and therefore is sung far too loud each time they get to it.

keenley *(adj.)*

descriptive of enthusiastic singers-by-ear in a community choir who don't always hit the note the composer had intended.

knossington *(n.)*

a singer in a choir who in less enlightened times would have been tapped on the shoulder and told to mime. *Knossingtons* bravely fend off the composer's intentions wherever possible, forging on and hunting down the holy grail, *The Tune*, at almost every turn, save for when their part *has* the tune, at which point they cleverly improvise a new tune, very close to the notes of the original.

sandsound *(n.)*
the swirling ball of sound, mushy and approximate around the target note, beloved of an infant school choir.

balmashanner *(n.)*
the *exquisitely* heart-warming feeling generated in the listener on hearing a choir of children, often engaged in *sandsound* (q.v.).

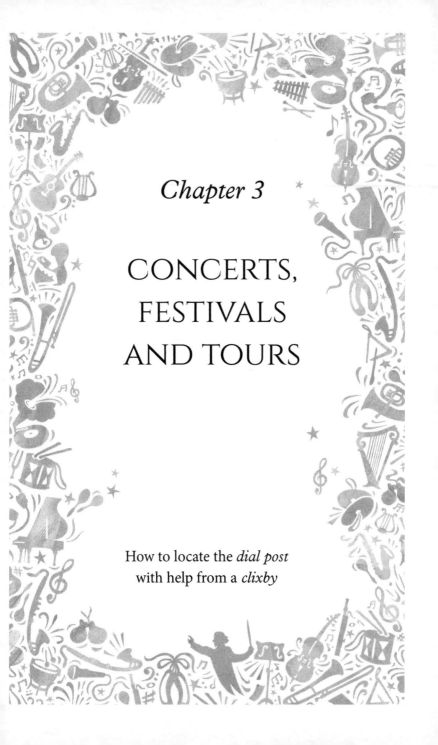

Chapter 3

CONCERTS, FESTIVALS AND TOURS

How to locate the *dial post*
with help from a *clixby*

sidley *(n.; pron. SY-dli)*

any of various types of wooden boards or panels, built into the internal walls of modern concert halls for acoustic reasons, rendering them a cross between a school physics lab and a 1970s sauna. Despite allegedly being fixable in hundreds of positions, they always seem to be in the same place.

hathersage booths *(n.)*

the original round Perspex and holed-chipboard booths, still remaining in some old concert-hall foyers, originally designed to hold telephones and now used to play music, programme details or children's educational materials in an amusing, faux-retro way.

limbrick *(n.)*

any manner of pre-purchased tile, nameplate, brick or token sold to sponsors specifically to allow them to put their name up in the foyer of a musical establishment, in order that others might know where they appear in the donors' pecking order.

wigfair isa *(n.)*

a private reception on the first night of a concert season held to pay tribute to investors and celebrities;

usually takes place in a roped-off area in full view of as many people as possible.

cold overton *(n.)*
a sad-looking foyer bar sandwich or salad that appears both ancient and unappetising but that has a price tag consistent with a meal at one of New York's finest, flights included.

gratwich *(n.)*
the sandwich in the concerthall bar that first impresses you with its presentation, then awes you with the wording of its contents on the artisan slate chalkboard, before finally astounding you with its price. See also *cold overton*.

kessock, north *(n.)*
the chap who shouts. ''Ow much!?' in a Lancashire accent in the foyer bar when confronted by the cost of two glasses of champagne.

kessock, south *(n.)*
the person serving the *north kessock* (q.v.).

keld *(n.; pron. KELT)*

a ticket left beside your interval drinks by bar staff, with your purchase helpfully itemised in the handwriting of a general practitioner.

boquhapple *(n.)*

food brought from home for consumption in the foyer of a concert hall, in order to avoid paying the extortionate prices of the concession cafe.

acton trussell *(n.)*

the folding table at the back of the foyer in a provincial concert hall where a visiting international artist is forced to sign copies of their latest recording for an implausibly small line of people, half of whom are front-of-house staff.

keward *(n.)*

the person whose job it is to wait next to the roped-off desk during a CD signing and allow one odd-looking, introverted, potential stalker in at a time.

stackpole elidor *(n.)*

a PR sleight of hand whereby the price of the cheapest seat in the house (offered once every twelve years, and which involves sitting in another room and watching proceedings via a small screen) is used to rebut charges of elitism, while the venue bar continues to charge £13.50 for a glass of house white.

deopham stalland *(n.)*
seat booked online for a suspiciously good price that proves to be on intimate terms with the loudspeakers. See also *cannon hill.*

totley rise *(n.)*
the absurdly tall steps in the cheap seats, high up in a theatre, sometimes requiring the use of oxygen.

cadoxton-juxta-neath *(n.)*
a seat that is very close to a raised stage at a concert, allowing its occupant to see the soloist's chin, the conductor's bum and the occasional flash up a cellist's skirt.

coppa view *(n.; slang)*
usher's term for a whole row of *cadoxton-juxta-neaths* (q.v.).

backmuir of pitfirrane *(n.)*
the nether reaches of an orchestra pit in an old theatre not dissimilar to the low seams of a Welsh mine.

brown candover *(n.)*
material used solely for hardwearing seat covers in
now-ageing concert halls and 1970s double-decker
buses.

buttsole *(n.)*
the small fold-down seat just inside the concert hall
used by ushers that squeaks during the quiet bits.

carlton scroop *(n.)*
the feeling of disenchantment experienced by a
growing queue of people thanks to the execrably
slow-functioning ticket-checker.

climping *(n.)*
the act of removing one quarter of a ticket before
allowing a person into a musical venue and placing
the stub on a spike.

clixby *(n.)*
person who counts people at a concert using a finger-

held tally counter (before writing down the number, placing it in their pocket and never looking at it again).

carlton in lindrick *(n.)*
a concert-hall ticket checker who is very friendly when you explain you need to get out briefly at the interval but who vows never to have seen you before when you attempt to regain entry moments later.

west bilney *(n.)*
the front-of-house chap who stands all night at the far fire-exit door, which has been unused by man or beast for forty-four years.

dial post *(n.)*
the spot in a concert-hall foyer, equidistant between the toilets and the emergency exit, where a decent phone signal is finally available.

duns tew *(n.)*
algorithm used by concert-hall architects to work out the time disparity per person between the interval queues for the ladies and the gents and, subsequently, the ratio of female to male toilets required during construction.

hedgehog bridge *(n.; slang)*
an indication of slowness, often used when referring to the pace of the ladies' toilets queue at the interval. Usage example, overheard at the Roundhouse, Camden, during the iTunes Festival: 'Babe, let's nip t' Monarch over t'road and use their loo. It's slower than t'*hedgehog bridge* in 'ere.'

johnby *(n.)*
the slightly sad figure whose job it is to help you to a towel in the bathroom of a high-end nightclub or concert hall and who expects a tip for doing so.

tarbet *(n.)*
the sad red-and-black plaid jacket left unclaimed every night from the concert-hall cloakroom.

blubberhouses *(n.; slang)*
term used in jazz circles for classical concert halls.

carthamartha *(n.)*
a tiny poster for a weekend music event affixed to the post of a traffic sign; generally written in such a small font that it is impossible to ascertain which of the words are (a) titles of songs, (b) DJs' names, or (c) travel directions.

hackness *(n.; colloquial)*
name given, by the few remaining locals, to the town of Thorpeness during the weeks of the neighbouring Aldeburgh Music Festival.

botwnnog *(n.; pron. boh-TWIN-og)*
a large, culturally diverse European city, particularly popular for its music festival, which has somehow managed to get itself twinned with a complete hole back in Blighty.

alsop-en-le-dale *(n.)*
a pet festival of a well-known conductor, which they run in their spare time.

barmby on the marsh *(n.)*
exclusively contemporary music version of an *alsop-en-le-dale* (q.v.).

glassonbury *(n.)*
any of the current crop of achingly trendy music festivals devoted to minimalist music.

camas luinie *(n.)*

a person who has been to Glastonbury every year since the festival started and insists on showing you their numerous scrapbooks to prove it.

odstock *(n.)*

nickname given to classical music branch of the Glastonbury Festival.

lostock *(n.)*

legendary bass festival that takes place in the Azerbaijani town of Baku (literally *basso*), where the atmosphere, at 28 metres below sea level, is thought to facilitate lower note potential.

appleby parva *(n.)*

a festival that manages to pull off a residency from a subsequently bemused world-class star who will perform to four members of the church flower-arranging committee and a verger, generally due to the world-class star's agent not having done their homework. See also *alsop-en-le-dale* and *barmby on the marsh*.

cannon hill *(n.)*

the location of the seats you managed to acquire for

a very reasonable price at the local outdoor summer picnic concert but which you discover, on the day, to be in a truly unfortunate spot vis-à-vis the cannons for the closing *1812 Overture*. Outdoor form of *deopham stalland* (q.v.) tickets.

gate helmsley *(n.)*
a man who watches from his garden, just down the road from the summer concert, as you take a good ten minutes to parallel park and remove your numerous picnic items, before pointing out that you're not allowed to park there.

field assarts *(n.)*
the people at an outdoor summer music festival who direct you to the nearest parking spot by chatting to each other assiduously.

goatacre *(n.)*
the measurement of distance between a recently erected, rural open-air concert stage, and the closest parking spot the touring orchestra's bus can find.

arscott *(n.)*

any summer music festival that attracts largely posh, often networking, corporate audiences.

gotherington *(n.)*

a gathering of people at a cool outdoor music festival who are listening to an orchestra play Rachmaninov because either (a) they thought *The Isle of the Dead* was a new band and decided to give it a go, or (b) The Sisters of Mercy are on next and it was worth it to get a good place.

wainfleet all saints *(n.)*

Lincolnshire-based tribute band who performed at the now-legendary Wood Not Stock Tribute Festival, alongside Light Purple, Washington ACDC and The Below Average White Band.

ffestiniog *(n.)*

a twelve-pack of beer or small 'party-pack' barrel carried around at festivals, doubling as a stool.

harpsden bottom *(adj.)*

descriptive of rear clothing that is creased due to having sat for hours at a festival on a shooting stick.

crofts of dipple *(n.)*
the pattern left on the thighs from using the picnic hamper as a seat at a summer concert.

ascott d'oyley *(n.; slang)*
picnic blanket taken to summer music festival, Glyndebourne, etc.

dewlish *(adj.)*
descriptive of the semi-damp state of a summer music concert blanket when unpacked at home later that night.

east looe *(n.)*
the particular festival Portaloo that is to be avoided at all costs.

jack-in-the-green *(n.)*
the original medieval practice of throwing a rubber chicken around the crowd at an outdoor concert – a game that usually starts in the hour or so before curtain up and often ends in the presence of a member of the St John's Ambulance staff.

fugar bar *(n.)*
old English type of early Kendal mint cake popular in the days of St Bede and used by players in need of added stamina at harp and song festivals.

carstairs junction *(n.)*
the location, after an outdoor concert, where you find yourself within a crowd of other hopeless cases, also burdened with cool boxes and blankets, who can't find their cars in the field car park, either.

heanton punchardon *(n.)*
the fading mark left by a festival hand stamp during the following week, when you wish to retain it to extend the memories.

cwm-miles *(n.)*
assessment of mileage done on musical tour when filling in an expenses claim later. One standard mile equates to just over two *cwm-miles*.

kirkton of cults *(n.)*
the small-town stop on the concert tour that is well known for being a bit League of Gentlemen and where no one ever stays over.

kirkton of largo *(n.)*
the small-town stop on the concert tour that is well known for its quietude and complete absence of audience.

kirkton of tough *(n.)*
the South Yorkshire leg of any tour.

kirktown of fetteresso *(n.)*
the small-town stop on the concert tour that is traditionally known to have the highest proportion of game audience members, keen to become groupies.

lower canada *(n.)*
nickname for parts of North Dakota, USA, bestowed by UK touring orchestras in recognition of their tougher audiences and the extended periods locals have endured without cultural visits.

cockshoot *(n.; slang)*
term used by string quartets for a well-paying gig. Thought to originate from bookings such as the Debutante Ball in the London Season.

dog village *(n.; slang)*
term used by touring orchestras for certain metropolitan stop-offs in Essex.

bedlinog *(n.)*
an over-familiar embrace exchanged between touring orchestral players last thing at night in the hotel to signal that they are up for something.

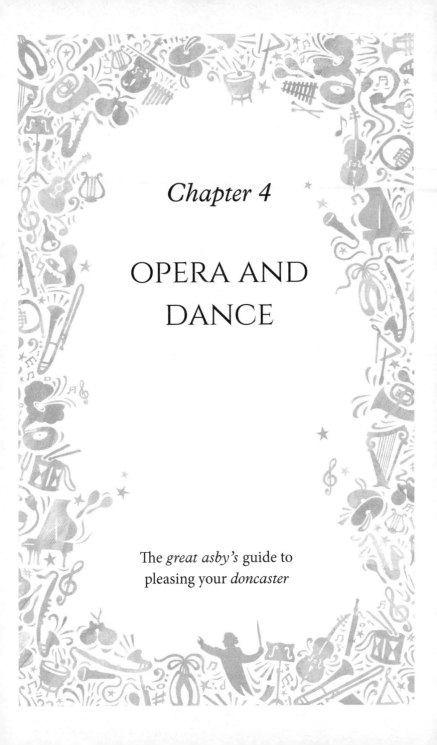

Chapter 4

OPERA AND DANCE

The *great asby's* guide to
pleasing your *doncaster*

gilfach *(n.)*

person who gens up on an opera plot before going to see it by visiting relevant websites and maybe even reading the odd book.

gilfachreda *(n.)*

person who gens up on an opera plot before going to see it by asking a *gilfach* (q.v.) what it's all about.

golden square *(n.)*

the pleasant chap you chatted to at the opera (and whom you put right on a few things about the genre) whose name you see on the next Forbes List, whereupon you learn he just happened to bankroll the opera you were watching.

goldhanger *(n.)*

the pointedly well-dressed sort often seen near a *golden square* (q.v.).

jamphlars *(n.; slang)*

the reddish orange corduroys worn by young-fogey opera-goers and prospective UKIP candidates.

cock alley *(n.; slang)*

the Crush Bar at the Royal Opera House, on a night with a high proportion of corporate clients.

hamp *(v.)*

to eat from a wicker case in between the acts of an opera.

hamperley *(adj.)*

well-to-do or affluent looking, occasionally corpulent. Often applied to those who *hamp* (q.v.).

hampnet *(n.)*

the password for the free wifi at Glyndebourne.

hampton lucy *(n.)*

the target demographic of many 'opera in the park' events, as revealed in an internal briefing document from Garsington: 'We appear to be fine with the broader *hamperley* types – it's the Mini Cooper-driving, city-living *hampton lucys* we need to target aggressively. Ad in *Tatler*? Thoughts?'

gardens, the *(n.)*

any of the series of outdoor operas that are good to

talk about but too expensive to attend such as Garsington, Grange Park, Longborough, and the grounds of Elton John's mansion.

dallam *(n.)*
the light above the upper tier of an opera-house circle that dims to a pleasant glow when the action commences.

ardnaff *(adj.)*
descriptive of the sound of some contemporary operas, which exemplify the eternal composer's dilemma: how to tread the fine line between wanting to shock and wanting one's music to be loved. Usage example, overheard in Crush Bar: 'I don't know about you but I haven't heard anything so *ardnaff* since *The Knot Garden*. Could've done with some secateurs to prune this one. And why is everything *bathed in green light*?'

childwall *(n.)*
chorus of children used on stage in opera to distract from the pain of the modern music and barren staging.

laity moor *(n.)*

a member of the chorus in an opera you spotted playing one part and now, three scenes later, is clearly playing another, disrupting your already limited suspension of disbelief.

bilton haggs *(n.)*

once acceptable terminology for female member of an opera chorus (pre-1900). Usage example, translated from the synopsis of Verdi's Il travatino ('The Tiler'): 'Groutio, the tiler, enters stage left and sings, "*Tu sei il collante che tiene insieme le piastrelle*", before exiting stage right, pursued by Don Idrualico and various *bilton haggs*.'

carnkie *(n.)*

the female chorus member in the opera crowd scene who's been in the company for years and who seems to suit the pseudo-medieval setting more than the others despite looking a little bit like Jimmy Krankie.

impington *(n.)*

singer who is often cast in a breeches role (a male part in the opera, traditionally played by a woman).

girdle toll *(n.)*

an algorithm used by opera directors, in conjunction with health and safety managers, to stress test the planned design concepts of a contemporary opera production, to see if it can be achieved without killing the overweight central star.

great asby *(n.)*

this year's opera starlet.

boxbush *(adj.)*

descriptive of the diaphanous fabric used by opera designers for the filmy garments worn by leading ladies in their bedroom scenes, specifically in order to give retired colonels and tired stockbrokers a lift. Usage example, overheard in Royal Exchange Jewellers, London: 'Used the corporate freebies to *Lucia* last night. I was late, then I fell asleep in the first act – but when I woke up, there was the soprano in her *boxbush* nightie. My word! Orso's was heaving afterwards.'

cynffig *(n.; pron. SINfig)*

costume worn by Maria Ewing during her run in Richard Strauss's *Salome* at the Royal Opera House in the

1990s, which she threw into the crowd each night, often hitting one of the front-of-house commissionaires.

bellasize *(n.)*
unofficial categorisation system of opera-house costume departments which read **S**, **M** and **LP**, said **to be** abbreviations for Elisabeth Schwarzkopf, John McCormack, Luciano Pavarotti.

furze platt *(n.)*
type of wig that comes pre-attached to a horned helmet, as worn by a Wagner opera character or stag party member.

geshader *(n.)*
a particularly violent Bayreuth opera hat.

gartsherrie *(n.)*
costume worn by opera chorus members in barroom drinking-song scenes, and modelled on those worn by Tiller Girls or women of ill-repute in a cowboy western movie.

bishopwearmouth *(n.; slang)*
a truly minor non-singing role in an opera, yet one

that allows the singer to wear a ridiculously lavish costume.

ballencrieff toll *(n.)*
the opera equivalent of the extraneous characters in *Star Trek* who beam down from the Enterprise with Captain Kirk only to be killed off. *Ballencrieff tolls* are minor extras who are not integral to the plot (and thus might not be there at the end) but who are vital for chorus singing and puffing out singers' CVs.

halton moor *(n.)*
the nickname of the principal character of Verdi's lost Yorkshire opera *Oh, t'Ello!*, in which a pub wench runs away to marry an exotic dry-stone-wall merchant.

badharlick *(n.)*
operatic laughing, as heard in the opening lines of 'Vesti la giubba', which is never funny.

skeffling *(n.)*
the art of exaggeratedly enthusiastic acting perfected by chorus members in the party scenes of operas, often with empty tankards in hands.

butteryhaugh *(n.; whole word pronounced 'bough', to rhyme with cow)*
the favoured gesture when two leading male opera singers meet on stage – it comprises a bow accompanied, on the descent, by a right-hand 'bouncing bomb' motion.

bilbster mains *(n.; French)*
the overused stage action in opera when a male villain creeps up on a female lead and envelops her chest from behind. Known as doing 'a Janet Jackson' in pop music (cf. the infamous September 1993 cover of *Rolling Stone* magazine).

hartsop *(n.)*
in opera, a character's swansong, intoned as they (a) take poison, (b) jump to their death, or (c) rush out under an avalanche.

bleddfa *(n.)*
the final notes sung before the death of an opera character or on the discovery of the death by others, as in the grief-stricken *bleddfa* of Rodolfo over Mimì's lifeless body in *La bohème*.

old basing *(n.)*
the style adopted when a classically trained opera singer 'does jazz'. Usage example, from the unpublished first draft of *The Fry Chronicles*: 'Cab to concert. American opera singer's attempt to sing jazz. Came out more like the *old basing* of a gung-ho sixth-former. Left at interval. Groucho. Home 3 a.m.'

stocker's head *(n.)*
name given to the moment, prior to the last act of an opera, when the conductor takes the applause. It is thought to be named for the amusing vision of the conductor's face above the pit wall, often with hand resting thereon, said to resemble a person in the stocks.

doncaster *(n.)*
alternative term for an opera director.

elephant and castle *(n.; slang)*
internal opera-house nickname for the last act of *Tosca*.

beltring *(n.)*
alternative name given to the 'Little Italy' area of the Hertfordshire town.

dinbych-y-pysgod *(n.)*

the first ever Welsh opera, based on the story of Orpheus and Eurydice, composer unknown.

eau brink *(n.)*

a state in which one finds oneself at Wagner operas in which it would be desirable to get to the lavatory swiftly – can arise at any time from ten minutes in up until the end.

ardfernal *(adj.)*

descriptive of the inner sections of Wagner operas, during which the vast majority of the audience is thinking only of the smoked salmon they will have at the interval.

germansweek *(n.)*

the period in which the restaurants around Covent Garden sell more *Wurst* than any other. Said to coincide with Wagner's 'Ring' at the opera house.

headlam *(adj.)*

when you appear, to all intents and purposes, silent, yet your *minterne parva* (q.v.) is playing the loud bit of a Wagner opera.

hockholler *(n.)*
person who shouts 'bravoruf' instead of 'bravo' in an attempt to convey that he once stepped inside the foyer of the Munich Opera House.

lunt *(n.)*
a particularly passionate ballet fan who comes to watch their favourite star armed with several armfuls of cut flowers, which they proceed to throw at the stage, leaning from the amphitheatre with only a smidgeon less awareness of their personal safety than they have accuracy for the target.

cannop *(v.)*
applicable to male ballet dancers; to half dance, half limp along behind a solo ballerina as she steals the limelight with her jumps.

follifoot *(n.)*
the occasional thwack of pointe shoes hitting a ballet stage, breaking the reverie to remind us that even awe-inspiring ballerinas are mere flesh and blood.

doonfoot *(n.)*

the somehow sad padding across the stage by a ballerina after performing her solo at a rehearsal.

kershopefoot *(n.)*

a walk characterised by the feet turned outwards, the natural gait of the professional ballet dancer.

tacolneston *(n.)*

ballet term for the moment a ballerina places her foot in her partner's lap to gain height.

hungladder *(n.)*

a ballet dancer so well endowed, his groin would necessitate crampons and breathing apparatus if one attempted to scale it.

cock and end *(n.)*

a dance often seen in rap and hip-hop videos from the late 1990s onwards, in which the male lead cannot refrain from checking himself and the female 'corps de ballet' appear intent on reversing into everyone.

hopton wafers *(n.)*

the bedrock manoeuvre of morris dancing, involving a run-up, a hankie waved in the face and a retreating cry of 'Heave my thigh-bell'.

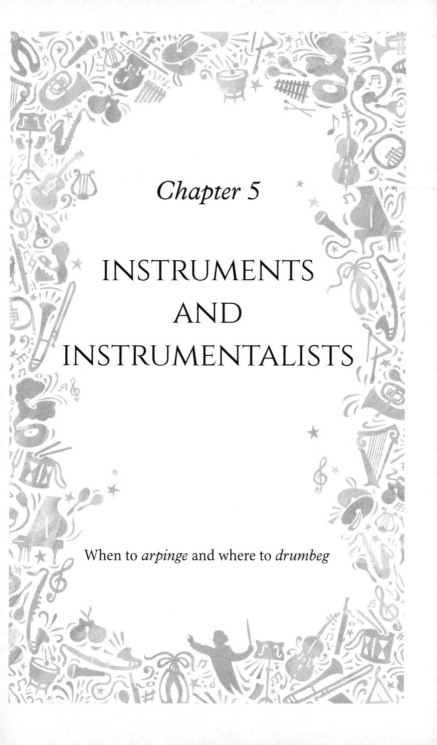

Chapter 5

INSTRUMENTS
AND
INSTRUMENTALISTS

When to *arpinge* and where to *drumbeg*

ible *(n.; pron. IBB-le)*
the musical instrument that is a ruler twanged on the
edge of a table.

allerton mauleverer *(n.)*
the position in which a music stand is left when the
previous user has been unable to fold the extending
upper sections back into place.

babworth *(n.)*
unit of light emitted by an ageing music-stand lamp,
equivalent to half a Swan Vesta.

brompton regis *(n.)*
a superior music stand a player has personally
invested in following a bad case of *backhill of clackriach* (q.v.)

tranarossan *(n.)*
a person clever enough to understand *why* some instruments transpose.

barton bendish *(n.)*
a manoeuvre performed on a theremin consisting
of an upwards and then downwards shift (similar to

that heard on the Beach Boys' 'Good Vibrations'), which, when botched, can give the impression that the Clangers have invaded your concert.

hinton ampner *(n.)*
the sinister rounded metal tube, made from a re-cycled kettle element, emerging from the side of a theremin.

drumbeg *(v.)*
to issue a request, in vain, as the course director at a county youth orchestra course, for players to stay back and help shift the percussion.

drumdollo *(n.)*
the member of a school steel-pan orchestra who is asked to play the pan that is struck only once every thirty-two bars.

drumblade *(v.)*
to spin around, for show, in a rest beat while playing steel pans, a move appropriated by the percussion section of the Simón Bolívar Symphony Orchestra of Venezuela.

framlingham *(adj.)*

descriptive of the sound of a tam-tam once struck.

upper bangor *(n.; slang)*

timpanist.

drumbuie *(n.)*

the sound of timpani when the tuning pedal is being
applied prior to a concert.

blair drummond *(n.)*

the proud, upright stance of a timpanist while playing
a particularly impressive solo, such as in *Also sprach
Zarathustra* by Richard Strauss, knowing that all eyes
are on them, in much the same way as a peacock
during courtship.

uyeasound *(n.; slang)*

artist's term for a vibraslap, the comical percussion
instrument.

fring *(n.)*

sound made on a vibraphone when a chord is struck
and left to resonate.

newbold on avon *(n.)*
the often overwhelming desire of all novice tubular-bell players to make the familiar two-note ding-dong of a doorbell.

belchamp walter *(n.)*
the fluffy 'barber's pole'-coloured section, near the bottom, of a bellringer's rope.

farleigh wallop *(n.)*
the sound of a flaccid bass drum struck during tuning when it has not yet been tightened.

drumsturdy *(n.)*
the brace that fits over a marching drummer to allow him to walk and strike a bass drum while sporting a fetching tiger skin.

runhall *(n.; pron. RUNNAL)*
a percussionist's run, during a performance, behind a line of varied percussion instruments, to reach the one they have to play next.

knab, the *(n.)*
a small, flat table, built on the base of an old music

stand and used by percussionists or Magic Circle entertainers to hold the smaller pieces of their kit, which they need to pick up in a hurry.

kittwhistle *(n.)*
the item used by the coxswain of a samba band, or *warse* (q.v.), which they appear convinced counts as a musical instrument.

warse *(n.)*
formal title for the coxswain of a samba band. The one with the *kittwhistle* (q.v.). Who appears to be unaware of how many of the crowd around him want him dead.

hunt's corner *(n.)*
the Spooneristic description given by a close-knit French horn section to the grumpy dep.

chevithorne *(adj.)*
descriptive of the winding tubing of a French horn.

bealachandrain *(n.)*
swivelling action used by French horn players to dissipate dribble around their instruments to the point at which they can use their *poole keynes* (q.v.).

horn ash *(n.)*
the sound made by blowing through a French horn when the *poole keynes* (q.v.) are depressed.

horneval *(n.)*
players' nickname for the little-known Florida French Horn Festival.

fazakerley *(adj.)*
descriptive of the tone of some trumpeters: meaning slightly tired-sounding and on the edge of flat.

lampeter velfrey *(n.)*
the half-drape, half-flag items that hang from the tubing of ceremonial trumpeters.

balsam *(n.)*
the collective term for any salve applied to trumpeters' lips, post-performance.

tooting graveney *(adj.)*
descriptive of the nerves experienced by trumpeters on 11 November at 10.55 a.m.

farthinghoe *(n.)*
technically correct term for the protruding slide section of a trombone.

saasaig *(adj.)*
descriptive of the state of having a sousaphone wrapped around the body. When a person is *saasaig*, their figure assumes a pleasing 's' shape and is irresistible to children.

catslip *(n.)*
red marks on a brass player's lips after a long practice session; may develop into full-blown *birdlip* (q.v.).

birdlip *(n.; slang)*
the effect on a brass player's mouth of a long playing session; so named for its slight resemblance to Daffy Duck. See also *catslip*.

coity *(adj.)*
descriptive of the curls and turns of the tubing of some brass instruments. See also *chevithorne*.

cauldcoats holdings *(n.)*
small sections of leather or faux-leather casing placed

on random tubing sections of brass instruments by players, in much the same way as geography teachers do with elbow patches.

cornist ganol *(n.)*
formal term for the absence of a brass player who hasn't made it back from the *crew's hole* (q.v.) in time to make his entry.

dreghorn *(n.)*
formal term for the tubing and funnel trick done by every brass player since time immemorial when visiting schools.

farsley *(adj.)*
descriptive of a brass note played by an instrument with too much moisture inside, leading to the impression that you are hearing Mozart played on a musical shisha pipe.

poole keynes *(n.)*
the small, often hidden valves on brass instruments that allow the players to blow out the spittle. The resulting expulsion of spray is considered by many brass players to be a charming addition to quiet string passages.

poolewe *(n.)*
the patch of liquid beside a brass player's chair, the result of using their *poole keynes* (q.v.).

hill of drip *(n.)*
the mound of gunk formed by the combination of brass players' spittle and their pile of tissues on the floor.

ayle *(n.)*
the mythical elixir of Talos, the patron god of brass players.

iken *(n.)*
the bluey-green, mouldy-looking tarnish that made school brass instruments so attractive.

kinghorn *(n.)*
the old-school member of the brass section who has never been reconstructed and always goes a little too far with the lippy, chauvinistic comments to the female conductor.

kirk of shotts *(n.)*
the legendary evening, still talked about with reverence among each year's fresher student brass intake,

when the Philip Jones Brass Ensemble recreated Bach's church at Arnstadt using full shot glasses and downed them all in the interval. As is still often overheard, stage left in the orchestra: 'The brass cats were howling *that* night!'

kirby overblow *(n.)*
the phenomenon that occurs when a brass dectet premieres a new work in the central nave of an echoey church and the second performance appears to take place in the side aisles just a few seconds later.

blore *(n.)*
the sound of low pedal notes played on brass instruments, not dissimilar to an old generator draining the last drops of water from a central heating system.

bachelor's bump *(n.)*
the stomach protuberance of many a brass player who, in the absence of a spouse to go home to, can be seen heading straight to the pub after a concert.

fant *(v.)*
of brass or wind players, to miss or fluff a note. Usage example, overheard in the green room of the Hallé

Orchestra, after a performance of Ravel's *Boléro*: 'Ok . . . who *fanted*?'

aykley heads *(n.)*
the phenomenon of wind and brass players' heads moving in tandem with their instruments, as if locked together by some secret force.

windlesham *(n.)*
a device consisting of a handkerchief or 'fluffy snail' on the end of a long string, used to send down the bore of a wind instrument to see if it can retrieve any unsavoury water-based friends.

doublebois *(n.; pron. DOOblaBWA)*
name given to the woodwind bumper who is the fixer's last option; the one who brings his dog and smells of old cardigans and Clan pipe tobacco.

nazing mead *(n.)*
the action of blowing a woodwind instrument on a note that manages to vibrate one's nostrils.

collamoor head *(n.)*
the thin silver tube that extends out of the top of a

bassoon, which looks as if it might be suitable for frothing milk in a cappuccino.

fagley *(adj.)*
descriptive of or similar to the tone of a bassoon.

farndish *(adj.)*
descriptive of the sound of a bassoon ensemble. Usage example, overheard at Music for Youth: 'Can we get a coffee? I've just heard a version of "Grace Kelly" by Mika. Played by thirty bassoons! It was just so . . . so . . . *farndish*, I need a sit-down.'

lower brockholes *(n.)*
the open sections on the bottom of a contrabassoon, which can be reached only by depressing about three feet worth of reformed silver cutlery masquerading as keys.

acaster *(n.)*
alternative term for principal oboe.

acaster malbis *(n.)*
the length of time a principal oboe can play a note for the orchestra to tune up before turning blue.

duckhole *(n.)*

secret finger hole on an oboe used to create the special sound needed in *Peter and the Wolf*.

little hautbois *(n.)*

technical term for an oboe reed that has been detached from the instrument in order to be blown through to annoy someone – see *nazeing* – or to produce that old favourite, 'Sweep's Lament', from *The Sooty Show*.

nazeing *(n.)*

the action of blowing through an oboe reed while it is not attached to the rest of the instrument. Usage example, overheard in the green room at Leeds Town Hall: 'If she doesn't stop *nazeing* right behind me, I'm gonna ram that reed down her cakehole!' See also *little hautbois*.

tuesnoad *(adj.)*

descriptive of any note played on a bass clarinet.

kilspindie *(n.)*

the extending spike protruding from the bottom of bass clarinets, both to make their keys accessible to performers and to turn them into instruments of war.

aunk *(n.)*

the scientific term, coined by Adolphe Sax, for the first note a student manages to get out of a saxophone.

harle syke *(adj.)*

possessing a mellifluous tone on the saxophone, applied particularly to altos and sopranos to suggest a soft, ethereal quality.

dumcrieff *(n.)*

the sound made by a flute choir.

purfleet *(adj.)*

descriptive of the shape of a flautist's lips during a performance.

elim *(adj.)*

descriptive of the sound of a piccolo.

doehole *(n.; slang)*

teachers' term for the first finger hole on a recorder.

bumble hole *(n.)*

the one hole on the back of a recorder.

brockholes *(n.)*
any of the finger holes on a recorder that, inexplicably, have two apertures close together rather than one. See also *bumble hole*.

preston bagot *(n.)*
the act of giving bagpipes a jolly good squeeze with your elbow while continuing to play the pipe with your fingers – the bagpipe equivalent of patting your head and rubbing your tummy.

pincock *(n.)*
any type of small wind device taken to football matches to toot until its owner is forcibly restrained by another spectator, prompting a round of applause from onlookers.

findhorn *(n.; pron. FINND-horn)*
the old kazoo that lives in the key drawer for no apparent reason, next to the dead batteries.

fringford *(adj.)*
descriptive of the sound made when sucking rather than blowing on a mouth organ.

hill of mountblairy *(n.)*
the name given to any mighty organ with a minimum of three manuals (keyboards).

blairingone *(n.; pron. BLAIRINgone)*
a piece of music played by the organist at the end of a service, as people hasten for the door; a chance to show off and a time to vent bottled-up energy after years of being scowled at by the vicar. Bum notes are consequently not merely tolerated but de rigueur.

capel ulo *(n.)*
the name of an ancient, some say secretive, branch of the Royal College of Organists who allegedly meet once in a blue moon to decide on new names for organ stops. The last time they met was supposedly in 1956 when the group was divided over the naming of a commemorative stop for legendary organ builder G. Donald Harrison. The resulting 'Hautbois Cacophonal' took four months to ratify.

fen drayton *(n.)*
a rare organ stop that adds a $1^3/_5$ folk effect to each note plus a simultaneous 'horse bell'. An acquired

taste for which organists often have to seek the vicar's permission.

glencarse *(n.)*
an undersized piano stool that necessitates reaching the hands upwards to play the keyboard.

fingerpost *(n.)*
the wooden section at each end of a piano keyboard that is just a tiny bit too small to balance your coffee cup on safely.

inchnadamph *(n.)*
the felt pad above a pedal on a piano.

lidget *(n.)*
the widget that lives inside a grand piano and holds up the lid, in order that a soloist can play too loudly. See also *lidgett*.

lidgett *(n.)*
the mini-me version of a *lidget* (q.v.) that lives inside the *lidget* itself and holds up the lid just a little, as preferred by the front-of-house staff.

langrick *(n.)*

a pen or pencil that has found its way past the piano lid and into the innards of the beast, which jangles in pain each time the strings on which it is lying are played.

llanrumney *(n.)*

the movement of the thumb down a piano keyboard, sounding only the black notes, for pleasure. Not to be confused with *kemble* (q.v.).

old blair *(adj.)*

descriptive of the sound made when some of your favourite music is played 'on the composer's very own piano', which appears to sound just like the one in the Fox and Newt, Burley Street, Leeds.*

peter's finger *(n.)*

the sensation experienced while playing an ageing piano when the finger comes into contact with the rough wood of a key that has no ivory veneer.

spelter *(n.)*

a short-to-medium-length passage during a piano showpiece that involves both hands locked together

* Centre of the known universe.

to play streams of fast-running octaves that would mesmerise an audience were it not for the frenetic wobbling of the pianist's double chin.

broadwoodwidger *(n.)*
a lock on the castors that, when engaged, prevents the grand piano from entering the cello section during a particularly energetic part of the concerto.

derwen las *(n.)*
the mysterious mechanical innards, named after their inventor, that turn pianos into pianolas.

acharacle *(n.)*
the smooth, lozenge-shaped buttons just above the keyboard on a piano accordion, none of which appears to be an off switch, sadly.

capcoch *(n.)*
the Saturday customer in the music shop who wanders from keyboard to keyboard pressing the 'demo' button.

langal *(v.)*
to sound a note on a cimbalom.

purston jaglin *(v.; archaic)*
the playing of the harpsichord.

arpinge *(v.)*
to complain about the amount of time spent tuning a harp.

arpafeelie *(n.)*
the tingling sensation felt somewhere between the spine and the cranium, brought on by the harpist's upward-running arpeggios just before the climactic chord of a great work.

harpurhey *(v.)*
to strum lightly up and down a harp, to create the film effect of 'We are now going back in time.'

ellingstring *(n.)*
the wisp of horse hair that flails from a violin bow during a concert until the soloist has a suitable rest in which to remove it.

chinnock *(n.)*
the chin rest of a violin which, when the violin is

placed on a flat surface, doubles as a place to keep small change.

babcary *(n.)*
the small, oval red patch on a violinist's neck formed by holding the instrument under the chin.

braeface *(n.)*
the tortured look used by violinists (eyebrows raised, mouth vaguely demonic) to signal that they *would* be in ecstasy if only they had chosen an instrument that did not have to be held in place using only their chin.

y fflint *(n.)*
the two f-shaped holes on the sound board of a violin that have always presented an irresistible challenge to schoolboys everywhere, hence the number of school violins clanking with contents such as small change, rubbers and, in extreme instances, a compass.

bridgemary *(n.)*
the traditional Space Invader pattern in which the bridge of the instruments of the violin family are carved.

halfpenny furze *(n.)*
the plush recycled furry-dice material that smells of ancient books and that is used to line old violin cases.

fiddlers hamlet *(n.)*
the arch-shaped section inside the top of a violin case containing resin, spare strings and half a packet of Polos.

ilfracombe *(n.)*
the ornate marquetry work on the fingerboard of a period stringed instrument.

ings *(n.)*
the viola version of 'dinner ladies' arm'.

ings, broad *(n.)*
a particularly nasty case of the above.

east sheen *(n.)*
the rich tone achieved when the cello section of an orchestra is on form.

baildon wood bottom *(n.)*
the small block, anchored to a chair leg during a concert, that allows cellists both to secure their spike and trip up stage hands during the interval.

east third *(n.)*
conductors' term for cello and double-bass section.

baddesley ensor *(n.)*
the near-permanent, indented lines in a guitarist's fingers, gained from frequent pressing on the frets; makes the fingers look not unlike Kaa from Disney's 1967 version of *The Jungle Book*.

bream's meend *(n.)*
the small, rubber-coated step on which a classical guitarist rests their foot to stop their guitar from sliding embarrassingly down their thigh during performance.

hoffleet stow *(n.)*
the angle at which a lute's pegbox is offset from its fretboard, allowing the player to prop it up on its own when nipping to the loo.

picklenash *(n.)*

the inescapably smiley, childlike sound generated by string players when they pluck their instruments en masse, an effect that has ruined many a solemn moment for an unwise composer.

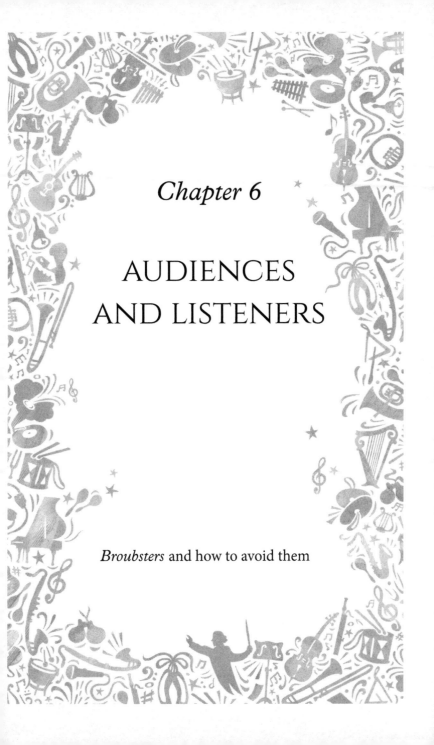

Chapter 6

AUDIENCES
AND LISTENERS

Broubsters and how to avoid them

auchenshuggle *(v.)*

to move your bag along the ground with your feet so as not to lose your place as you inch forward in a queue for returns at a sold-out concert.

fancott *(n.)*

a small stool used to save a space in a ticket queue by a determined music lover.

carleton forehoe *(n.)*

person in a ticket queue who annoys everyone by leaving their case in their stead and going off for coffee.

ingrave *(n.)*

person who accepts free tickets to a sold-out music event and then declines to go when the night comes round, despite having nothing better to do.

talywain *(n.)*

the untimely feeling of fatigue you experience when you have had tickets for a musical event for some time but, a few hours beforehand, creeps over you, making you feel as though you can't be bothered to go. Not to be confused with *ingrave* (q.v.).

geocrab *(v.)*
to sidle aimlessly around in or just outside a concert-hall foyer while talking on a mobile, oblivious of real-world events or people.

arabella *(n.)*
a young woman, aged between thirteen and seventeen, usually home-schooled, who has been dragged to an opera or concert by her family and forced to wear her best frock. See also *gunthorpe*.

gunthorpe *(n.)*
a male version of an *arabella* (q.v.), often identified by tweed jacket, bright tie and Polyveldt shoes.

cuckoo tye *(n.)*
a mad-looking, spotty dickie bow sported by a mad-looking, spotty music student who has been home-tutored and likes to attend Bruckner concerts, with score.

dorking tye *(n.)*
the semi-mystical rules, formulated in the Surrey town in 1889, that dictate how a concert bow tie must be fastened. Usage example, overheard at

a Bullingdon Club dinner, Chalgrove, 1986: 'Now look, Seb: we may be drunk; we may be coked out; we may be eating from the navels of the finest call girls this country can offer; but I must still . . . invoke *dorking tye* rules. Get that bloody bow sorted!'

cornard tye *(n.)*
a dickie bow that has been tightened so much, it cannot be undone. See also *cuckoo tye*, *dorking tye*.

compstall *(n.)*
the conspicuous-looking person in jeans and T-shirt amid the tuxedos and pearls of the posh seats, leading people to surmise they have not paid for their ticket.

beardly batch *(adj.)*
descriptive of the type of audience attracted to the 'commuter music' chamber performances in the foyer of the Barbican – many of whom have come all the way from Shoreditch.

jemimaville *(n.; slang)*
an audience overpopulated by Chelsea residents. Usage example, from Harrison Birtwistle, diary:

'First night of *Minotaur*. Tony did me proud. The odd jeer from from *cock alley*, but nothing heavy. Afterwards, ventured to check out the work done on the Cadogan. It was pure *Jemimaville*. Can't wait to get back up north.'

beckermet *(v.)*
to 'venue drop'; that is, to make clear that one has had personal experience of one of the world's great musical venues, often by over-authentic pronunciation of its name. Although the Met is a popular choice, the most favoured name to *beckermet* is Bayreuth.

cultybraggan *(v.)*
to go on at length about the one time you met a young Luciano Pavarotti coming out of the gents in Llangollen.

appin *(n.)*
the act of googling a concert programme before attending, in order to impress others by passing off the knowledge as if plucked from the air.

apperknowle *(n.)*
someone who displays too much insight into an

obscure work, thus exposing themselves as having indulged in rather too much *appin* (q.v.) before a concert.

elmley lovett *(n.)*
the piece of music you to claim to love beyond all others, and about which you wax lyrical at length, but which was in fact the one you studied at A level and which you use in every grown-up conversation about music, hoping not to be found out.

delnamer *(n.)*
someone who bluffs a little too much about their classical music knowledge and unwittingly bestows a rather comical new moniker to a staple piece of the repertoire, such as *The Well-Tempered Clavicle* or *Also sprach Zaragoza.*

clammerclough *(v.)*
to feel so unconfident about the pronunciation of a certain composer, title or venue that one falls silent each time it becomes unavoidable in conversation, e.g., 'I love that aria . . . in the Donizetti opera, the one Pavarotti sings, called, umm . . .' Pause. 'Are they new shoes? Oh, they're lovely.'

cadnam *(n.)*

an abbreviated name for a piece of classical music (such as *Così* for *Così fan tutte*), which you have heard people use on countless occasions but which you are too nervous to adopt because the one time you did (saying *Burana* for *Carmina Burana*), everyone stared at you. Other popular ones used by *fogwatts* (q.v.) the world over include: *Mastersingers* (for . . . *of Nuremberg*), *The Rite* (for . . . *of Spring*) and the less commonly explained 'Yah!' (for 'Yah, you're absolutely right, I am a pillock!').

chilthorne domer *(n.)*

a person who has never understood what it is about the natural horn that people like but has always been too polite to say so.

kelloe *(n.)*

a smile exchanged between two people in the concert bar, half hopefully, before both their partners show up.

ipstones *(n.)*

the background noise, a mixture of murmuring and grumbling, made by a queue as its component members shuffle slowly towards the concert-hall entrance (derived from i.p.s. measurements, inches per second).

islesteps *(n.)*
the halting, shuffling movement made when, tickets in hand, one's concentration is split between walking down the auditorium steps and trying to make out the row labelling.

legsby *(n.)*
a particularly belligerent patron of a theatre or concert hall who will not budge an inch to enable you to move past them to reach your seat. Not to be confused with a *grindiscol* (q.v.).

grindiscol *(n.)*
a type of *legsby* (q.v.), who pretends to be helpful by means of smiles, muted exhortations of 'Not at all' and even the odd feigned action, but who is, in fact, not budging.

buttsash *(v.)*
to wave one's posterior in someone else's face when arriving late to one's seat, often due to the seated

person in question refusing to budge one inch from their position on the moral high ground.

bonson *(n.)*
a Z-list celebrity attending a concert who, despite reaching their seat in plenty of time, will not sit down until the very last minute in order to be seen by as many people as possible.

gorstage *(n.)*
the area immediately in front of a stage that has been kept as a VIP area and that is consequently only sparsely populated as many of the freebie-swilling glitterati had better things to do.

compton chamberlayne *(n.)*
a row of reserved seats at a school concert that are filled at the last minute by various rotund bigwigs, one of whom is wearing a chain of office, and accompanied by a bowing and scraping deputy head.

atlow *(n.)*
the 'golden' level, usually achieved with a beanie or similar, that means your head apparel will not block or even be noticed by the audience member behind you.

atch lench *(n.)*

the notional level accepted by Birmingham Symphony Hall staff as being that which is acceptable for the person in the seat behind to see over. See also *atlow*.

attercliffe hilltop *(n.)*

the hat-bedecked idiot seated in front of you at a concert who doesn't give a monkey's whether you can see or not.

gwernogle *(v.)*

to move either left or right during a concert or opera in order to be able to see around the *attercliffe hilltop* (q.v.), in front of you.

atrim *(n.)*

guerrilla action taken in extreme circumstances by person seated behind an *attercliffe hilltop* (q.v.).

atworth *(n.)*

the concert usher who will insist that all headgear is removed so as to keep all the audience happy and prevent any outbreaks of *atrim* (q.v.).

high row *(n.; pron. 'row' as in 'cow')*
when it all kicks off in the cheap seats.

cranage *(n.)*
action required when sitting in restricted-view seats.

upper vobster *(n.)*
a school child in the grand tier of a concert venue who unsettles everyone else by appearing permanently on the verge of spitting on the people below.

bunny hill *(n.)*
one of many internal nicknames for an opera house's amphitheatre section. Also known as *crazies hill* or *deaf hill*. See also *zeal monachorum*.

zeal monachorum *(n.)*
a particularly shifty-looking group on *bunny hill* (q.v.) who all arrived separately but now appear to act as a group in order to spook the front-of-house staff.

emsworth *(n.)*
unit of light emitted by the exit signs above concert-hall doorways, sufficient for you to be aware of them all the way through the concert, but insufficient to

prevent you falling arse over tit when you need the loo in a long piece.

cleobury mortimer *(n.; pron. MORE-timer)*
your internal musical body clock, which tries to keep track of your progression through a multi-movement work so that (a) you can regulate your bladder, (b) you can monitor your partner's likelihood of dropping off and, most importantly, (c) you don't look a complete arse by clapping in the wrong place. See also *achalone*.

pizien well *(n.)*
the slow motion wave of semi-nausea that rises from the stomach when, despite having felt sure you had already counted two short breaks in a three-movement work, you suddenly hear a definite stop and the start of the middle movement, thus meaning your *cleobury mortimer* (q.v.) is out by at least thirty minutes and you didn't even order interval drinks.

portinscale *(n.)*
the often involuntary hand movement made while listening to piano music and feeling compelled to play along: a kind of table-top, air piano.

bachymbyd *(n.)*

a well-known church melody that Bach incorporates at a quarter speed in the bass line of a work, to which you foolishly start to try to sing the words in your head.

spixworth *(n.)*

the measure of disappointment felt when film music is transferred to the concert-hall stage and you re-alise that far more than half your pleasure was due purely to the visuals. Concerts of video-game music are measured in *tera-spixworths*.

cardewlees *(n.)*

people who have to bite their lip, raise their eyebrows, and occasionally leave the hall in order not to giggle during a performance of serious contemporary music.

cardigan island *(n.)*

the person who takes a score to a concert and hums select passages, resulting in a small collection of empty seats around them.

ceciliford *(n. pron. cecil-I-FUD)*

a *cardigan island* (q.v.) who now brings his score to a concert on a tablet.

iping *(n.)*

the sounding of a small bell-like sound, to denote that you have not remembered to turn off your phone before sitting down to the concert.

lower badcall *(n.)*

the sounds made by your mobile going off while you are sitting in the good stalls seats at a concert.

upper badcall *(n.)*

as *lower badcall* (q.v.) but when you are in the choir seats and immediately fixed with the death-ray gaze of the conductor and three thousand audience members.

scrabster *(v.)*

to frantically scramble; a motion enacted by a concert-goer when they realise the ringing phone that has just ruined a glorious moment for two thousand people is theirs.

malcoff *(n.)*

the thoughtless clearing of the throat by an audience member, which comes in the middle of a *goldstone* (q.v.), leading to a pair of raised eyebrows and forlorn look from the conductor, and a request for a refund from other members of the audience.

cofton hackett *(n.)*
the particularly nasty cough, more death rattle than mere bark, that irritates everyone during a concert, especially as its owner appears to perform their own whooping cadenza during the quietest part of the slow movement.

kinlet *(n.)*
a small child or baby who, measured in physical terms, is a mere fraction of the size of the orchestra's brass section but who, measured in decibel levels achieved in the middle of the concert, appears to be beating them hands down.

warkworth *(n.)*
a concert-goer whose constant shushing of others is the one thing that really puts everyone off.

deepweir *(n.)*
state of passive calm adopted during the interval at a contemporary music concert, before everyone is prepared to let on that they didn't understand it either.

horton-cum-studley *(n.)*

the loud man in the box at the Albert Hall, who drinks champagne at the interval, sits on the ledge and thinks he's it.

buscot *(n.)*

small semi-circular plastic widget that fixes to the side of a plate to hold a wine glass, allowing the holder the all-important freedom to make mad gestures of delight over the first half's music with their fork.

bigods *(n.)*

people who buy amphitheatre tickets but come all the way down to the ground-floor bar at the interval, mainly to star spot, before having to race to get back to their seats before the music starts.

jaywick *(v.)*

to wander, unfairly, in pairs in front of someone who is in the queue for interval ice-cream, all the while conversing loudly and pretending you hadn't noticed they should be before you.

keighley *(adj.; pron. KEITHly)*

descriptive of the stranger who gets talking to you

in the interval about his journey to the venue, the nature of the current market in his chosen profession – invariably insurance – and the numerous occasions on which he has heard today's music performed so much better.

housay *(n.)*
idle gossip overheard in the interval bar and recycled as gospel.

broubster *(n.)*
the type of bounder who steals other people's interval drinks.

cuckoo's corner *(n.)*
a gathering of people at a performance of the 'Ring' Cycle who bring their own sandwiches and eat them cross-legged in a circle on the floor of the foyer.

compton pauncefoot *(v.)*
to slip sheepishly into an empty seat in the *compton chamberlayne* (q.v.) for the second half of a concert.

nether poppleton *(n.)*
a bankable piece of music, considered one of the

greats by the public, that is placed towards the end of a concert to retain the audience. A genuinely fine *nether poppleton*, such as *The Lark Ascending*, can keep an audience present and attentive despite even the most challenging of *staynalls* (q.v.).

ardtoe *(n.)*
a game played inside your shoe (flicking your big toe and the toe next to it against each other to create a small 'thwacking' sound); usefully employed when the music at a concert has become so dull you start to flick the rhythm of 'Her Name Is Rio', while singing it in your head.

yorton *(n.)*
a badly disguised closed-mouth yawn common at the 'Ring' Cycle; makes the perpetrator appear to be gurning.

downies *(n.)*
a momentary lapse of consciousness in a concert seat, revealed via several descending nods. Usage example, overheard in Bristol's Colston Hall bar: 'Quick, get that coffee drunk and I'll get you another. Three times I caught you having *downies* back

there – and the third time, you were snoring!' See also *dowlish wake*.

elberton *(v.)*
to nudge gently, mid-concert, at the first hint of *downies* (q.v.).

inverkip *(n.)*
an inadvertent public nap, characterised by the head falling back, the mouth open, the tongue out, and a crowded concert hall all around.

heads nook *(n.)*
a resting place on which to snooze at a concert, sometimes an unwitting stranger's shoulder.

invermoidart *(n.)*
the result of a sudden involuntary lunge, which pulls the subject out of a deep *inverkip* (q.v.), and, in so doing, sends a small dribble of spittle flying onto their neighbour.

jacks hatch *(n.)*
a violent snort that wakes you from your in-concert snooze, attracts maximum attention and makes you

a talking point at the interval. Depending on the conductor, it could also attract a *hadlow stair* (q.v.).

dowlish wake *(n.)*
the post-*downies* (q.v.) period in a concert hall when one has woken after nodding off, characterised by a furtive discussion with your partner about whether you were spotted by fellow concert-goers. Not to be confused with a *jacks hatch* (q.v.).

lewknor *(n.)*
a person who saves up for expensive front-row tickets to a concert for a piece they have longed to hear for years and then, near the end, as the music begins to reach its climax, picks up their shopping bags and leaves for their train.

golden balls *(n.)*
the moment, just after the golden silence following the end of a superbly performed piece, when many male listeners finally unclench their buttocks.

beggearn huish *(n.)*
the moment at the end of a piece when conductor and soloist, both in taut, eyes-alert stance, are determined

that, despite the piece being ended, applause shall not start. Not to be confused with *goldstone* (q.v.).

goldstone *(n.)*
the point, during a particularly magical *beggearn huish* (q.v.), when the unbroken moment allows you to hear a combination of silence and your own tinnitus.

borve *(v.)*
to cry bravo loudly during the *beggearn huish* (q.v.) presumably in the mistaken belief that the sound of your voice is as much sought-after as that of the international artist on stage. Usage example, from Adrian Boult's letters: 'The performance went well. GH [Holst] said it was a marvellous premiere, marred only by that cad in the second row who was *borving* like an arse every five minutes.' See also *clapworthy*.

fivepenny borve *(n.)*
similar to a standard *borve* (q.v.) but used in jazz circles after a particularly good solo which the *borver* wants to be a part of.

clapworthy *(n.)*

the member of an audience whose mission in life it is to be the first to applaud at the end of a musical work, partly to spoil the mood but principally to prove to others that he knows it has ended. See also *borve*.

upper clapton *(n.)*

a particular type of applause that involves stretching out and lifting the arms away from the body, usually while still in one's seat. It is used as both (a) a halfway house when you can't be bothered to join a standing ovation, and (b) to signify you are clapping and, somehow, meaning it more.

friskney eaudyke *(n.)*

the person wearing beads and a patchwork beanie hat you got talking to in the concert interval, whose initial chattiness you mistakenly found refreshing and whom you now are at pains to avoid on the way out.

chaddlehanger *(n.)*

person who attempts to gain unauthorised access to the after-show party at a classical spectacular concert by pretending to be a member of G4.

brunatwatt *(n.)*
the nervously twitching man with plastic bag and gift-wrapped box who hangs around the stage door at Bayreuth.

brymbo *(n.)*
the heavily made-up woman in loud stilettos who hangs around the stage door at the Welsh National Opera.

bryndioddef uchaf *(n.)*
memorabilia collected by fans, often *brymbos* (q.v.), usually obtained at concerts, book signings and other encounters. Examples range from the rare and priceless 'Used Jar of Jussi Björling's Hair Cream' to the extremely common 'Pair of Russell Watson's Sunglasses'.

ullock *(n.)*
a person who manages to get onto a stage in the first ten minutes of a stadium concert, resulting in a nervous glance from the lead singer, a triple rugby tackle from the security guards and a short stay in A&E.

dungworth *(n.)*

rock band term for a person who shouts out the names of obscure album tracks as requests in between songs, mainly to show off that they know them.

dunge *(n.)*

crowdsurfing that results in an elbow in the eye for one or more audience members.

up sydling *(v.)*

technical term for crowdsurfing.

lumb *(n.)*

the state your ears are in after leaving an extremely loud rock concert where you chose to stand too close to the speakers.

drefach *(v.; slang)*

to burst an eardrum.

fulking *(v.)*

hanging around the DJ at a disco, thinking up requests he doesn't want to play and you don't want to hear, just to be around the DJ.

gardiffaith *(n.)*
person who will gladly make enemies by telling their neighbours to turn the music down on Sunday afternoons, all summer long.

golfa *(n.)*
someone who whistles inane, one-note, non-tunes while playing eighteen holes.

knockglass *(n.)*
someone who simply doesn't get minimalist music.

aberargie *(n.)*
a person whose route into classical music started after hearing the Royal Philharmonic Orchestra playing 'Does Your Mother Know'.

cerrig man *(n.)*
PR demographic term for the type of person who is most likely to buy classical music when it is mixed in among tracks from Elbow, Belle & Sebastian, and Jeff Buckley.

clunie *(n.)*
a classical music fan who has latched on to one

particular star, usually still living, as being the greatest singer ever known, despite plenty of evidence to the contrary.

glencoe *(n.)*
affectionate name for the passionate (possibly bonkers) band of Glenn Gould aficionados.

folksworth *(n.)*
a person who rants about how no one appreciates the wonders of folk music any more, while simultaneously complaining that new folk bands make the genre too popular for its own good.

flodigarry *(n.)*
Shakespearean term for a muso hipster.

fogo *(n.)*
the vaguely anachronistic chap in the office who wears check jackets and dickie bows, who started the Wednesday Lunchtime Madrigal Group that no longer meets, and who shops at Past Times for his Secret Santa presents.

fogwatt *(n.; pron. FOAG-wat)*

a young classical music fan who dresses in the style of the landed gentry, talks like Alvar Lidell, and would love it to be 1920 again.

duddo *(n.)*

the member of the University Challenge team in the knitted tank top and bow tie who has been brought along solely to answer the classical music questions and sits through the rest of the programme trying to look as though they know the answers but have just been beaten to the buzzer each time.

bellochantuy *(n.)*

the feeling of beneficence experienced while listening to Gregorian chant, drinking Shiraz and reclining in a comfortable chair.

little mancot *(n.)*

a type of comfortable chair installed in a male den or shed, ostensibly for the purpose of listening to music in comfort but in reality loved for its sleep-inducing properties.

collingbourne ducis *(n.)*

a person who has a music 'everything' (from a music notepad bearing the legend 'Chopin Liszt' to a music umbrella, complete with notes from the 'Raindrop' Prelude). Surprisingly, most *collingbourne duces* (the plural form) are innately unmusical. In this respect, they are the equivalent of that well-known school sports phenomenon: the kid with the greatest kit and the least talent.

frotoft *(v.)*

to play a favourite track endlessly on repeat. Usage example, overheard in Tetley Bar, Leeds University Students' Union, 1983: 'Oh yes! Someone's put "Comfortably Numb" on! I remember *frotofting* this when it first came out and watching Why Don't You with the sound down.'

lerwick *(n.)*

a line of a song that has been so regularly and chronically misheard that the new version becomes the accepted one. Usage example, (not) from Queen's 'Bohemian Rhapsody': 'Spare him his life from his Wall's Sausages.'

upper nobut *(n.)*

a person who plays you their favourite music in the hope that you will love it too and, when you don't, insists on playing it again at higher volume. The musical equivalent of talking more loudly to foreigners.

wrabness *(adj.)*

the air of self-confident smugness inspired by a love of a little-known musician whom others will only find interesting when they sell out and transfer to a major label in a couple of years time.

pilleth *(n.)*

legendary Swansea punk outfit who, judging by the number of people who claim they were there, did their last gig at Wembley Stadium rather than the snug of The Three Ravens in Sketty.

hearn *(v.)*

to pretend not to have heard a particular piece of music you would rather not have to insult. Usage example: 'Gosh, did you hear that awful new piano album Paul sent with the composer playing twelve pieces based on each month of the year?' 'No, I *hearned* it – I said I'd been away in a Mongolian prison.'

waddicar *(n.)*

any piece of music kept in the glovebox that induces a nostalgic singalong from the whole family but which often bewilders new passengers.

cardrona *(n.)*

the free CD of classical favourites given out with a Sunday newspaper, which never leaves your car's glove compartment and is mostly used to scrape the ice from the window on a frosty morning.

chipstable *(n.)*

a scratched or cracked CD that lives in your car and is entirely useless yet somehow never finds its way out of the car and into the bin.

gargunnock *(n.)*

the small blob of hardened matter that is sadly now permanently attached to your favourite in-car CD.

carfury *(n.)*

the small sprite that lives in your car's CD player and likes to ruin your favourite music at random moments.

garrabost *(n.)*

type of CD sold for £2.99 in motorway service sta-
tions that contains all the hits you love but mainly in
live versions that sound awful.

chidden *(n.)*

a hidden piece of music on a CD, partly intended to
appeal to superfans but mainly designed to scare the
living daylights out of you.

frith *(n.)*

the fleeting, transitory guilt felt (just before clicking
the play button) when using a free online streaming
service that pays minuscule royalties.

salters lode *(n.)*

any song that pops up on your digital music player
when it's on shuffle, which you swear you never
downloaded and must have been put there by a
younger sibling.

upper framilode *(n.)*

any song that appears at the top end of a search result for an artist on a digital music player but which,
on further investigation, turns out to be not by the

artist for whom you searched but an instrumental cover by a Peruvian panpipe ensemble.

exceat *(n.)*
the tinny sound emanating from another person's headphones.

st clears *(n.)*
ridiculously oversized headphones that would be mistaken for construction-site ear defenders were it not for the addition of a designer label and the deduction of several hundred pounds from one's bank account.

cefn golau *(v.)*
to break wind while listening to music on headphones.

cefn-coed-y-cymmer *(v.)*
to break wind while listening to music on headphones in a fellow student's room, thus ruining any chance of intimacy.

minterne parva *(n.)*
similar to one's inner monologue, the *minterne parva* is the medical term for one's inner orchestra, which

is never out of tune and provides the (internal) soundtrack to many a dull moment.

earswick *(n.)*
technical term for an earworm. See also *catbrain*.

innerwick *(n.)*
an earworm played by one's *minterne parva* (q.v.).

catbrain *(n.)*
the state you are in when the *earswick* (q.v.) you have been been plagued with all day has still not gone away and you are forced to resort to strong drink.

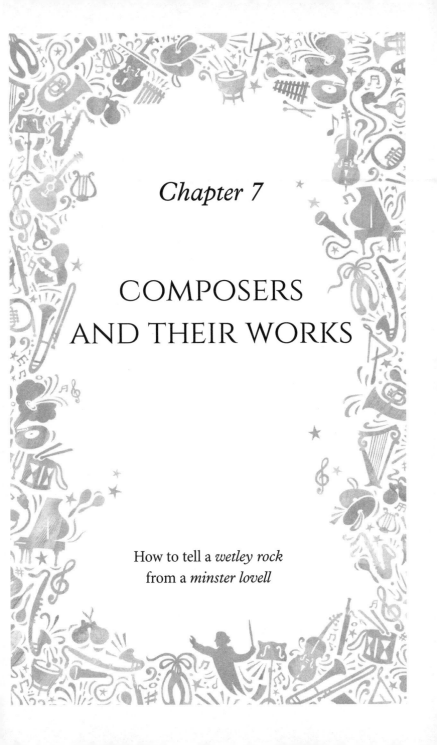

Chapter 7

COMPOSERS
AND THEIR WORKS

How to tell a *wetley rock*
from a *minster lovell*

boundstone *(v.; pron. BUN-stun)*
to leap enthusiastically from the audience on to a stage. Specifically used of modern composers to describe their haste to take a premiere's meagre applause.

bage, the *(n.)*
the school of twenty-first-century piano composers who followed in the wake of Einaudi by producing easy-listening keyboard motifs, worked up into three-minute pieces, somewhere between unpublished youthful Satie and Emeli Sandé.

inkerman *(n.)*
a composer who continues to favour fountain pen and manuscript paper over Sibelius music-notation software.

fovant *(n.)*
a musical charlatan who manages to spin sixth-form composition techniques into 'atmospheric piano moods'.

hook bank *(n.; slang)*
composer's notebook.

gilcrux *(n.)*

the feeling of resentment felt by a living composer when the only piece of theirs that the public has taken to its collective heart is the one where they were deliberately pastiching someone else.

hooke *(v.; pron. hookEE)*

to take time off from musical composition by prevaricating with distractions, such as mapping out bar lines several pages ahead, making previous sections neater or googling 'composers and their cats' on the internet.

ashby cum fenby *(n.)*

the person responsible, in a music-publishing house, for liaising with the company's living composers – the ones who *aren't* dead and *aren't* out of copyright but who *are* six months late with their new work.

kedlock feus *(n.)*

a game played in cars whereupon you have until the next set of lights to be the first to name the composer playing on Classic FM.

hoo st werburgh *(n.)*

the one member of a group of composers, such as 'Les Six' or 'The Mighty Handful', that no one can recall when trying to reel off the names.

arnish *(adj.)*

sounding a little like sub-baroque music and, therefore, similar to Thomas Arne. Often applied to the works of Maurice Greene, Carl Abel and Michael Nyman.

nymet tracey *(n.)*

a person whose name has become associated with a piece of famous music, often (though not always) through patronage, and, as a result, becomes a household name for generations to come. Classic *nymet traceys* include Sigmund Haffner, commissioner of Mozart's 'Haffner' Serenade; Rodolphe Kreutzer, violinist behind the Beethoven 'Kreutzer' Sonata; not to mention Joy Mangano and her miracle mop, subject of Beethoven's famous Ode.

anton's gowt *(n.)*

catch-all name for any ailment musicologists believe might have prevented a composer from completing their final masterpiece. With Mozart, it was a dodgy pork cutlet; for many others it was syphilis; and for poor Bruckner, it was an addiction to fine cheese and wine.

arinachrinachd *(n.)*
pseudonym of Karl Jenkins's lyricist.

barabhas iarach *(n.)*
the real name of Karl Jenkins's lyricist.

gadfa *(n.)*
allegedly the first word of Shostakovich's daughter, Galina.

llong *(n.)*
infamous headline from the *Evening Standard* after the classic 1986 Welsh National Opera production of Wagner's 'Ring' Cycle.

fyvie *(adj.)*
nervousness experienced by conductors during a performance of Sibelius' Fifth Symphony as they near the last six bars' hammer-blow chords.

canon bridge *(n.)*

the thankfully long-lost Stokowski middle section of the Pachelbel, which switches key and moves into waltz time, arranged for triple orchestra.

whitchurch canonicorum *(n.)*

the standard wedding repertoire of most string quartets, which, by canon law, must include Pachelbel every fifth piece.

canon frome *(n.)*

the heady, near-hysterical sensation experienced by string quartets at weddings as they launch into the Pachelbel for the umpteenth time at the request of yet another *canon pyon* (q.v.).

canon pyon *(n.)*

someone who approaches the wedding string quartet and asks them to play the Pachelbel, seemingly oblivious to the fact that it is currently being played.

high easter *(n.)*

reference to the Easter of 1991, which holds the record for the highest number of performances of Handel's *Messiah* in the UK.

bac *(n.)*
nickname given to the unfinished Cantata 552b, 'Mein Gott ein starker Kaffee ist', by Johann Sebastian Bach.

arnol *(n.)*
a mythical piece of music by Sir Malcolm Arnold, the great British composer, said to be for orchestra and washing machine, with stylophone obbligato, and allegedly unfinished at the time of his death.

draycot foliat *(n.)*
mythical Mozart manuscript, believed to be a set of early variations, written during the composer's trip to the UK and based on the bawdy folk song 'Long Funny Dingle-Dangle'.

tyrie *(n.; pron. TEE-ree-ay)*
the missing movement of Mozart's so-called 'Swiss Mass', written on the 'Fondue Tour' of 1789.

einacleit *(n.)*
nickname given to some of Hummel's serenades because of their closeness to the music of Mozart.

egremont *(n.)*

nickname given to some of Hummel's overtures because of their closeness to the music of Beethoven.

joppa *(n.)*

an amusing aside made by a radio presenter, usually about the 'Trout' Quintet, which in fact is neither amusing nor, when you think about it, aside.

ballogie *(adj.)*

descriptive of the countless neglected marches of Sousa, the Strauss family or even Alford, with titles such as 'The Italian Rifleman's Jogging March', 'The Flick-Fluck March' or 'The Grand Gasworks Inaugural March'.Usage example, from *Father Tom and the Thief of Tuscany*: 'Sweltering in the Siena sun, he stared over the line of his spectacles and glanced down to his fobwatch. The mayor's train was now forty-three minutes late. As the town band continued to play all manner of *ballogie* pieces, Father Tom consoled himself by counting each bead of sweat that dripped onto the trumpeter's mute.'

easter ardross *(n.; slang)*
Stainer's *Crucifixion*.

anstruther easter *(n.)*
dodgy piece of Victorian English music rehabilitated to fit into a programme alongside the Stainer *Crucifixion* at a local concert.

staynall *(n.)*
a piece of music, often new or perhaps just 'challenging', that the concert promoters deem must be placed in the first half of a concert for fear that, if it were in the second, no one would bother staying. Usually used in conjunction with a *nether poppleton* (q.v.).

persondy *(adj.; pron. per-SON-dy)*
descriptive of a musical that seemed vivacious, exciting, energetic and generally fun but from which you cannot whistle a single tune.

alisary *(n.)*
any piece of classical music that has become known by another name, often due to schoolboy jokes. Common examples include 'Garlic Dressing' ('Gaelic Blessing') and *Best Pair of Nylons (Blest Pair of Sirens)*.

arford *(n.)*

any classical music title containing a double entendre that cannot be ignored. Purcell's 'When I am laid in earth' is a popular example, as is Walton's *Touch her soft lips and part*, closely followed by Henry Fictious's classic *Prithee do not spurn my ars nova*.

fugglestone st peter *(n.)*

official hymn tune name for the music adapted to the words of ''Twas on the Good Ship Venus'.

heol las *(n.)*

official hymn tune name for the music adapted to the words of 'Four and Twenty Virgins'.

ayres of selivoe *(n.)*

a collection of songs from which all but the first few lines appear to have been lost to the mists of time. The *ayres of selivoe* include 'Auld Lang Syne', 'God Save the Queen' and the 'Macarena'.

barber's moor *(n.)*

the remainder of the oeuvre of any composer who is famous for one piece, but whose other works have not reached popular acclaim.

booker *(v.)*

to *booker* someone is to make clear to them that the one piece of printed music they wish to buy is available only as part of a huge tome that costs the earth.

spindleside *(n.)*

the revolving sheet-music stand in a music shop, which must, by law, include 'The Entertainer' by Scott Joplin, 'Angels' by Robbie Williams, and a dog-eared copy of 'Chi Mai' by Ennio Morricone.

easter quarff *(n.)*

the type of long, twentieth-century organ voluntary that is played at the end of the Easter Sunday service and which you suspect contains many bum notes but you just can't tell for sure.

heaven's door *(n.; slang)*

crematorium staff term for 'My Way' sung by Frank Sinatra, due to its prevalence in services.

totscore *(n.; slang)*

orchestral parlance for works during which children can be expected to cry, such as *Peter and the Wolf*, *Babar the Elephant* or Boulez's *Pli Selon Pli*.

france lynch *(n.)*

the fumbled tune to the sixth and seventh lines of the French National Anthem that even the French don't know.

bimbister *(n.)*

a modern march, usually for wind band, which has echoes of many other more famous marches trapped inside it.

detchant *(n.)*

official hymn tune name for the group cry, beloved of placard carriers and protest marchers the world over, adapted to the words: 'What do we want? Blank, blank! When do we want it? Now!'

drummond *(n.)*

official hymn tune name of the music beloved of jogging military units, adapted to the words: 'I don't know but I've been told [*echo*]. Blank blank blank blank blank blank blank [*echo*]. I don't know but it's been said [*echo*]. Blank blank blank blank blank blank blank [*echo*].'

gallt melyd *(n.)*
official hymn tune name for the music adapted to the words of 'Oggy Oggy Oggy'.

wendons ambo *(n.)*
official hymn tune name for Rogers and Hammerstein's 'You'll Never Walk Alone'.

boughton monchelsea *(n.)*
any classical melody that has reached the football terraces and been blessed with new, occasionally obscene, lyrics. Examples include: 'La donna è mobile' ('Jose Mourinho'), 'Simple Gifts' from *Appalachian Spring* ('Carefree CFC') and even the old standard 'Guide Me, O Thou Great Redeemer' ('Who's the Bastard in the Black?').

flixborough *(n.)*
a piece of classical music whose film-music association has become so pronounced that it is more often referred to by the movie name than the original. Today, many orchestras are frequently regaled by requests for well-known *flixboroughs*, such as: 'Can we have the *Elvira Madigan*?' or 'Play the theme from *2001*' and even, 'Oi, sing that

bit from *Shawshank* where he locks himself in . . . come on!'

buldoo *(n.)*
a faux-Scottish work of light music purporting to 'evoke the sights and sounds of the highlands' (written years ago originally for a film about farming and kept in a bottom drawer ready to be rebranded when the opportunity arose).

ingleby barwick *(n.)*
official hymn tune adapted as *The Archer*s' theme, when played in its full-length accordion version.

thorpe arnold *(n.)*
official hymn tune name for the music to the Classic FM jingle.

minster lovell *(n.)*
the piece of classical music inserted into a politician's list of favourite music by their PR team, which they profess to have adored since childhood. See also *wetley rocks*.

wetley rocks *(n.)*
the pieces of pop music desperately inserted into politicians' personal favourites lists, by themselves, for credibility purposes. See also *minster lovell*.

jarvis brook *(n.)*
a piece of rock music that has been arranged for orchestra by a former pop star in a 'first for classical music', often with added unconventional features (usually a beatboxer) enabling it to be described as 'groundbreaking' by the *Guardian*.

newton poppleford *(n.)*
a piece of classical music which has been used, and occasionally abused, as the basis for a pop song and that now, no matter how hard you try, always brings said song to mind. Some of the finest bores in the world are those who go on at length about this: 'There it is. Can you hear it? There. No wait. *There*. "All by . . . my—self". There. Did you hear it? Ooh, and again . . . "All by . . ." Hey. Where've you gone?'

hoober *(n.)*
a song written about someone, the identity of whom

the composer has vowed never to reveal. The classic *hoober* is 'You're So Vain' by Carly Simon.

hoo meavy *(n.)*

a song written about someone, the identity of whom the composer has vowed never to reveal, but which everyone is confident they know anyway. The classic *hoo meavy* is also 'You're So Vain' by Carly Simon.

Chapter 8

MATTERS
MUSICOLOGICAL

Chilmarks, carlton curlieus and
other assorted *furneux pelham*

foxlydiate *(n.)*

mythical lost mode, said to have been that used by Sir Lancelot to woo Guinevere and subsequently banned by King Arthur.

cowley peachey *(adj.)*

descriptive of the delightful pastoral passages in much of Edwardian English music, prior to the horrors of 1914.

ampney crucis *(n.)*

the post-rationalised structure found in a famous piece of music by academic analysis, which can lead the discoverer to posit a hidden agenda and result in a lucrative side-line on festival panels.

idrigill *(n.)*

a type of madrigal that appears, on the surface, to be the height of cultural politesse but which is, in fact, all about shagging. A large proportion of madrigals are, in fact, wrongly labelled *idrigills*.

cross of jackston *(n.)*

musical marking denoting a section of piano music that doesn't need crossed hands to play, but that looks good if you do.

black torrington *(n.)*
a passage of music where a human with two hands is expected to play notes written for someone with at least four (often includes a *black notley* section, q.v.). Much favoured by Rachmaninov and Liszt.

black notley *(adj.)*
descriptive of a difficult passage of music, dense with crotchets and quavers. Usage example, from *Horrid Humphrey and the School for Aliens*: 'Just one week after his triumphant "pass" in Grade 3 piano, Humphrey arrived at his piano lesson and was confronted with his brand new Grade 4 pieces. They were unfamiliar and so *black notley*, he felt almost physically sick. He decided there and then to skive off next week's lesson to play Minecraft.' See also *black torrington*.

farleys end *(n.)*
Rock Ending No. 255, which involves the end chord repeated over and over again, with head nods, until a final *staccato* chord is sounded and the drummer adds one bass drum kick by mistake.

frampton end *(n.)*
Rock Ending No. 257, which is one huge chord,

followed by a long drum section, an expectant pause, then one more final chord, before all musicians smile in relief.

fala *(n.; pron. fa-LAR)*
two chords, the first short, the second long, usually appearing at the start of a piece; the musical equivalent of a 'Tadaa!'

troan *(v.)*
to warm up the voice with a scale to the word 'me'.

falahill *(n.)*
the section of a Christmas carol where one or two syllables are repeated over and over again in descending sequence, usually ended by the phrase 'in excelsis deo'.

south mimms *(n.)*
term for a large number of long, tied notes, often seen at the end of a piece when the last note is held for an inordinate length of time. The *south mimms* in Wagner's now lost fifth opera in his 'Ring' Cycle, *The Rise of the Norns*, was said to have lasted some twenty-four minutes, and have had the marking '*Bis die Bastarde schlafen gehen*'.

ayres quay *(n.; archaic)*

a unique key, distinct from any of the standard twenty-four recognised by most musical theorists. Today, it is beyond rare, although can still be favoured by (a) modern atonal composers and (b) first-round singers on *Britain's Got Talent*.

high flatts *(n.)*

pianists' name for the key of D flat, favoured by many as the richest-sounding of the keys and yet indistinguishable from the others in blind tests.

keycol *(v.)*

to flip up the loose ivory veneer of an old piano keyboard in an idle moment to make a percussive sound (an effect called for in Cage's *Time Out of Fashion*, for prepared piano and unprepared Scout).

edgebolton *(n.)*

the bottom right corner of a score that has been folded over ready for turning.

edgewick *(n.)*

the rapid turn of a page achieved by a pianist's page turner after (a) a dubious length of time spent blocking the page from sight with their arm and (b) a frantic nod from the pianist.

giosla *(adv.; Italian)*
musical term for 'in style of a satnav voice'.

vachelich *(adv.; German)*
musical term for 'to be sung in the style of a cow'.

halvosso *(adv.; Italian)*
musical term for 'to be sung in the style of an ocelot'. Rarely used.

carlton curlieu *(n.)*
formal term for the treble clef.

chilmark *(n.; slang)*
informal term for a pause symbol, one of the *furneux pelham* (q.v.).

furneux pelham *(n.; archaic)*
term for anything from the 'rests' family (literal translation, 'restraining furniture', from medieval French). All bar lines, pauses (e.g. *chilmarks*), ornaments and accents come under the umbrella of *furneux pelham*.

flourish, the *(n.)*
formal term for the bass clef.

kingslow *(adj.; pron. king-SLOW)*
orchestral musicians' term for too slow – roughly
three times slower than *adagio*. Usage example, heard
whispered at a performance of *Spiegel im Spiegel*: 'My
word, this is . . . *kingslow!*'

foxbar *(n.)*
any one bar of a different time signature to its neighbours, placed in a piece by a contemporary composer
to test performers and justify the commission.

pityme *(n.; pron. PI-time)*
the time signature a piece (usually a national anthem) is said to be in when it has fallen out of sync,
resulting in some horrendous *lagness* (q.v.) between
the soloist and the crowd in a stadium, pre-match.

connah's quay *(n.; slang)*
musical director's term for the key that is deemed the
only one suitable for an actor to sing in when doing
a guest spot, but that then renders the song all but
un-singable for everyone else.

tallentire *(v.)*

musical marking instructing the performer 'to play with talent'. Now very rare and only used to confuse.

back rogerton *(n.)*

a handwritten note, left in the margins of an orchestral score by a previous conductor, to warn of a difficult section of the piece and, more pertinently, the old duffer at the rear of the string section who always screws it up.

clapton in gordano *(n.)*

Italian musical marking for the smattering of applause, mixed with conversation, reserved for the leader of the orchestra's exit from the stage at the end of the evening, often interrupted by the stage crew coming the other way.

fegg hayes *(n.)*

the genre of music involving the use of words such as 'diddle', 'fol-de-rol' and, most of all, 'nonny'.

fotheringhay *(n.)*

an exponent of *fegg hayes* (q.v.)

freefolk *(n.)*

the mid-1970s scene in San Francisco, started by Ornette Coleman (prompted by his little-known liking for Steeleye Span), which produced such classics as 'Yo Spanish Ladies', 'Lavender's Blue, Baby' and 'I'll Go No More A-Reefin''.

flecknoe *(n.)*

the increasingly popular electronica 'Trance-Flageolet' music scene springing up in the hip Norfolk–Hoxton corridor.

new tolsta *(n.)*

any type of new music that you have never heard of before and, indeed, on the basis of the name itself, doubted to be real when your offspring told you about it. Examples of *new tolsta* include splitter-core, chap-hop, clownstep, folktronica, black midi, slayhammer and danger music. (NB, one of those *is* made up.)

mottisfont *(n.)*

a term for musical words whose spelling and pronunciation are sufficiently ambiguous as to put off the less brave. When faced with having to choose between rosin and resin, many opt for safety and the maxim: 'If in doubt, leave it out.'

hopesay *(v.)*
to deliberately mispronounce musical words, in your head only, in the hope that doing so will aid remembrance of their spelling, i.e. saying *p-sarm* for 'psalm'. The key part of this definition is 'in your head only'.

grovesend *(n.)*
a nugget of classical music info which, for some reason, you have always been able to recall and which has got you out of several sticky conversational situations. Usage example, overheard in Hot Numbers cafe, Cambridge: 'All the dons were there, waxing on about *Sturm und Drang* and the Enlightenment patrons – it was a nightmare. Then I remembered this thing I'd read about Goethe's *Prometheus*. Such a *grovesend*! Think I got away with it.'

figheldean *(n.; pron. FIGGLE-dun)*
a person who refuses to name a piece of music without mentioning its corresponding opus or catalogue number. See also *yr hob*.

yr hob *(n.; pron. WIRE hob)*

a person who insists on only using opus or catalogue numbers in place of their more standard titles. A conversation with a *yr hob* can be rather like a game of Battleships where only one person has sight of the board. Statistically, most *yr hobs* are also *somersal herberts* (q.v.).

somersal herbert *(n.)*

a person who insists on using the original language when referring to the title of any piece of music, thus making conversations a little like a chapter of Beowulf. Statistically, most *somersal herberts* are also *yr hobs* (q.v.).

high nibthwaite *(n.)*

somebody who understands all the rules of fugue.

Chapter 9

MUSICIANS
IN TRAINING

Transforming the everyday *grumbla*
into a fully fledged *garker*

bapchild *(n.)*

the tiny, moon-faced, well-heeled treble who sings the opening verse of 'Once in Royal David's City' at the Christmas service.

chub tor *(n.)*

the boy chorister who is never asked to sing the first line of 'Once in Royal David's City'.

cadole *(v.)*

to push a son or daughter into demonstrating their limited prowess on an instrument in front of guests.

gawber *(n.; slang)*

buskers' term for a small child who will stand and stare for hours but whose parents will not contribute a penny.

deeping st james *(n.)*

a relative's much loved party piece (often involving spoons) that is called for at every gathering and, after much protesting, performed to universal acclaim. See also *faverdale*.

faverdale *(n.)*
a relative, usually an aunt, who sings at family events
as a matter of course and is beloved by her relatives,
but whose personal 'sound' might leave newcomers
a little bewildered. Not to be confused with a *deeping
st james* (q.v.).

levalsa meor *(n.)*
a dance undertaken at a wedding where a young man
takes to the floor with a member of his family, usually an aunt, very much under duress.

vowchurch *(n.)*
a piece of music sung during the signing of the
marriage register by a friend of the couple, above an
appreciative hubbub.

fort augustus *(n.)*
the enthusiastic volume regularly achieved by well-
dressed people at a wedding during 'Jerusalem'.

haltwhistle *(v.; pron. HOLL-twissle)*
to place one finger over the pursed lips of a friend
who loves to whistle, in order that they might remain
a friend.

grumbla *(n.)*
a person who will never sing in public chiefly because they still remember, in their youth, a misguided music teacher resting a hand on their shoulder and telling them to mime.

goose eye *(n.)*
the manner of singing with wide eyes in order to show displeasure. For example, if one's relative begins to sing a descant during a carol at Christmas in a packed service, the goose eye may be the only course of public action short of pretending to faint.

dent *(v.)*
to sound out a tune on one's teeth, using the mouth cavity for pitch.

humber *(n.)*
someone who enters a room, nervously humming the vague remnants of a tune, and then says 'What?' before anyone has asked them a question.

irby upon humber *(n.)*
the sound of a portly *humber* (q.v.), whose natural heavy breathing adds a wind-machine effect.

humbleton *(n.)*

someone who is prone to humming tunes even though they don't actually know them.

hummersknott *(n.)*

the rare occasion when two or three *humbletons* find themselves sitting close together. Not to be confused with a *cardigan island* (q.v.).

wymering *(v.; pron. WIMMER-ing)*

to sound a tune by whistling while breathing in.

tapnage *(n.)*

the technical term for the sound of fingers drummed on a surface in rhythm to the radio, driving colleagues insane.

fortuneswell *(n.)*

person who knows only *sections* of a piece of music, which they then hum or sing loudly when that section occurs. Occasionally they attempt to sing beyond the bits they know, to bemused looks from friends and/ or ridicule from offspring. Not to be confused with *halsinger* (q.v.).

halsinger *(v.)*

to sing along to something without fully knowing it and therefore stick to belting out with gusto only the lines you know well enough. Not to be confused with the approach of a *fortuneswell* (q.v.).

kemble *(v.)*

to play a couple of notes in the bass area of a piano as you walk past while someone else is practising on it, just to annoy them.

smug oak *(n.)*

a person with perfect pitch who insists on telling you what key the fridge is humming in.

harmeston cross *(v.)*

to annoy people by singing the harmony to a song while in public, not just because you can but because you can't not.

welsh hook *(n.)*

the chorus of 'Land of My Fathers', for which everyone joins in, regardless of nationality (though they usually have to sing nonsense words).

y bala *(n.)*

the jaunty few notes in the middle of the Italian national anthem that are the instrumental bridge between two sections yet are always sung by the crowd at a rugby international.

llan-rhudd *(n.)*

official hymn tune name of the music adapted to the words of 'My Grandfather's Clock' when sung on a rugby team bus.

beeford *(n.)*

one who cries while on television during the singing of their own national anthem. The classic *beeford* is usually pictured standing between one team member who isn't singing and one so short only their hair appears on camera.

shafton two gates *(n.)*

the excited double take done at sporting events when spectators in the crowd see themselves singing the national anthem on the large screen.

lagness *(n.)*

a specific type of delay, often experienced in a sports

stadium, where one or more parts of the crowd are singing different parts of the same song, resulting in an unpleasant woozy feeling experienced by the TV-viewing public. If left untended, it can morph into *brympton d'evercy* (q.v.).

each end *(n.)*
the sound resulting when a form of *lagness* (q.v.) has got out of sync not once but twice with different parts of the stadium, and sounds like a CIA brain-washing tape.

brympton d'evercy *(n.)*
the result of serious *lagness* (q.v.), or occasionally *each end* (q.v.). In its purest form the noise will continue un-abated, forming a seemingly infinite spiral of the same song that theoretically could continue for ever, leading some post-Hawking enthusiasts to posit what is now referred to as the Infinite Singing Bear Stadium effect.

scarrington *(n.)*
a person who isn't so bad at karaoke to merit trip-ping up on the way to the mic, but not so good as to merit them having been up there for four songs now, blocking that little girl waiting to sing 'Let It Go'.

bangor-is-y-coed *(n.)*

an in-school workshop given by a junk-instrument orchestra or trash-can stomp group where enthusiastic enjoyment (rather than the chance to miss lessons) is genuinely the chief reason for taking part.

backhill of clackriach *(n.)*

the sculptural entanglement of metal formed when a number of old-style music stands have fallen over in a school music store room.

antony passage *(n.)*

the sound emanating from any practice room when a student is trying to master a particularly difficult section of a work. First used when the original two-piano versions of Brahms's *Variations on a Theme of Haydn*, played by Brahms and Clara Schumann to test out the score, went tits up at the *Vivace* section.

easton-in-gordano *(n.)*

a medium-sized house in pleasant grounds in Italy, France or Spain that advertises its week-long, summer music courses in the back of *The Lady* magazine.

elsing *(v.)*

playing music that you like and know but don't need to practise. It is thought that between 70 and 80 per cent of the practice time of most under-16s is spent *elsing*.

summerscales *(n.)*

an expression used by music teachers to refer to instrument practice that is less than fully committed, shall we say. Playing *summerscales* often involves a child picking up their instrument, playing a piece they mastered for an exam some time ago, then piping up 'Finished' six and a half minutes later.

exminster *(v.)*

to go completely blank in an early-grade music exam.

screeb *(n.)*

the language in which the comments for your Grade 1 piano exam appear to be written. Also used by GPs.

drumguish *(n.)*

the anxious feeling felt by percussionists in a university orchestra around ten minutes before the end of a rehearsal, when they remember that they will

have to move all the timpani into a storeroom, three
floors down.

tunnyduff *(n.)*
the catch-22, 'Forth Bridge' situation faced by directors of school ukulele ensembles whereby no sooner
have you tuned the last ukulele than the first ones are
out of tune again.

dalton piercy *(n.)*
a music teacher who tries to prove their youthful credentials by addressing everyone as 'guys', piercing
one ear and professing a misguided fondness for the
Kings of Leon.

glenduckie *(n.; slang)*
a larger-than-life, ever-cheerful person attempting
to bring classical music to any particular stratum of
underprivileged youth; thought to have been coined
in the tougher areas of Glasgow in the 1970s. See
also *glenmavis*.

glenmavis *(n.)*
a type of mother hen who has worked for many
years in the field of youth music in Scotland and

is always 'gobsmacked at the amount of talent in these kids'.

coed-talon banks *(n.)*
the frequent visits of classical crossover agents to music colleges, as they trawl around for the next Bond.

cadger path *(n.)*
the area immediately surrounding a busker within which one must look suitably appreciative so as not to appear uncaring or uncultured, and yet not so appreciative as to warrant putting some cash in the instrument case.

garker *(n.)*
mediocre amateur opera singer who includes the words 'sings at Covent Garden' on their website but forgets to add the words 'underground station'.

bell busk *(n.)*
a singer of serious opera arias, with acoustic accompaniment, in a shopping square.

bell common *(n.)*
type of 'popera' music sung by a *bell busk* (q.v.) when

the serious stuff has failed to attract sufficient coinage.

bell end *(n.)*
unaware shopper who walks across the patch of a *bell busk* (q.v.), throwing them off their performance.

horwood riding *(n.)*
the obligation to play in a small band, unsmiling and miserable, while on a moving float in a street parade, surrounded by disappointed children.

castle camps *(n.)*
a group of *castle tumps* (q.v.) paid by a National Trust house to act as 'period minstrels' to enhance your visit and 'bring the history of the building to life' (usually to be spotted on their smartphones in the cafe later in the day).

castle tump *(n.)*
singular of *castle camps* (q.v.).

cwm-byr *(n.)*
pejorative term for someone out of their comfort zone, e.g. a country bumpkin in the city, or an Einaudi-level pianist attempting Rachmaninov.

old cryals *(n.)*
the oldest of the veteran members of a philharmonic chorus.

lower altofts *(n.)*
sopranos who hide in the alto section for as many years as necessary, because they don't want to bother with the high notes.

stiffkey *(n.; pron. STU-kie)*
a fiendish key, avoided by amateur pianists. F sharp is the ultimate *stiffkey*, and has been known to result in hospitalisation when insisted on by visiting vocalists.

facit *(n.; pron. FAkit)*
a feeling experienced by amateur groups of singers or instrumentalists during the 'note-bashing' phase of learning a piece.

cornet's end *(n.; slang)*
term among brass-banders for a particularly fiendish test piece.

standlake *(n.)*
the bespoke banner adopted by brass bands that adorns their music stands.

cottenham *(n.)*
material traditionally used to make a *standlake* (q.v.).

dassels *(n.)*
the small fronds at the base of a *standlake* (q.v.).

cornsay colliery *(n.)*
the name of a fictitious band traditionally entered into every brass band contest, for luck.

fickleshole *(n.)*
a person who professes a hitherto unmentioned love of classical music just before their first appearance on a classical radio station. Not to be confused with *swaffham prior* (q.v.).

swaffham prior *(n.)*
a celebrity who reveals a genuine, hidden talent for classical music, usually Grade 8 in a particular in-strument. The proper place for this revelation is a weekend broadsheet article entitled 'My Homelife',

accompanied by a picture of them next to their Aga. Not to be confused with *fickleshole* (q.v.).

acton turville *(n.)*
any member of the local amateur dramatic or G&S society whom the others suspect is only in it for the costumes. If recent estimates are to be believed, this applies to around 90 per cent of the company.

balloch *(n.)*
the dressing-down given to an am-dram society chorus at the dress rehearsal in order to get the first performance up to scratch.

banc-y-darren *(n.)*
a worthy local arts project, which is so obscure and inclusive, it surprises all by beating the Royal Opera House to a much sought-after slice of Arts Council funding.

llansamlet *(n.)*
a unique and interesting project that receives public funding chiefly to tick regional political boxes. So called after the legendary Welsh Shakespeare Company production of an all-male-voice-choir

version of *Hamlet*, set in Rhyll, which changed the most well-known soliloquy to 'Look, I'm not being funny or anythin' . . . but to be or not to be . . . which is it?'

Chapter 10

TRIVIA AND TREATS

Everything from avoiding *towie*
to coping with *tushielaw*

henley down *(n.)*

the collective sigh of relief when the boss of the Arts Council has finally moved on from your venue and gone to take in the good work being done by the Ellesmere Port Museum of Shoes.

henllan amgoed *(n.)*

as per *henley down* (q.v.) but in Wales.

darenth *(n.)*

internal Arts Council measurement, an algorithm of both financial and artistic worth.

iscoed *(n.)*

the intern at an arts organisation who becomes incredibly popular because they fix everyone's computers.

hand and pen *(n.)*

simile used in arts-funding world, in the manner of carrot and stick, to suggest that if one has gone too far – with begging hand – the benefactor might not write the cheque.

govig *(adj.)*

descriptive of the behaviour of a culture minister whose chief talent is to alienate all the arts bosses he meets. Usage example, overheard in the ICA bar: 'This new chap . . . thought he was a bit . . . *govig* at first, but he seems to be going down rather well.'

kinbrace *(v.)*

to shake the hand of someone just a little too strongly and for just a little too long, usually to make a point; very common among record company A&R bosses. Not to be confused with the actions of a *knucklas* (q.v.).

grimsay *(n.)*

a stock 'talking head' used in a two-way interview on a morning news programme to talk down the government's arts policy.

knucklas *(n.)*

a particularly violent exponent of the *kinbrace* (q.v.), which leaves you with pronounced white marks and, at worst, a dislocated finger.

kilmahumaig *(n.)*

a dry, soulless contributor to a late-evening arts show

who can be relied on to provide the gloom to everyone else's cheer.

woolfardisworthy *(n.)*
any musical 'talking head', used in a three-hour-long TV special of the '100 best [insert musical theme here]', who seems to remember every moment of some long-forgotten decade like it was yesterday and whose motives you suspect are primarily financial.

stelling minnis *(n.)*
the algorithm used by TV news teams to reduce the amount of footage shot at a local music event to the four seconds eventually used in the piece on that night's programme.

zouch *(n.)*
an unexpected, electric pause left by a radio interviewer who receives an obnoxious answer from a bad-tempered musician under orders to promote a project but who would clearly rather be in their hotel bed.

killiecrankie *(n.)*
a particularly pessimistic, often poisonous, classical music critic.

lamlash *(n.)*

to receive a bad review in a very minor magazine; such as getting one star from *Twinkle*.

hacklet *(n.)*

older name for music blogger.

gubblecote *(n.)*

a person who, every once in a while when they can't think of anything better, pens a broadsheet rant bemoaning the death of classical music. The first *gubblecote* was thought to be J. F. Rochlitz writing in the *Allgemeine musikalische Zeitung* in 1798.

byton hand *(n.)*

journalists' term for an interview given by a classical music star on joining a stage musical or releasing their first album of dad rock, in which they profess never to have liked classical music in the first place.

knypersley *(adv.)*

in the manner of a classical music critic.

jolly's bottom *(n.)*

the article a music journalist is expected to write as

part of the quid pro quo for that weekend to see *La traviata* in Verona, all expenses paid.

doffcocker *(n.)*
a journalist who prints the words of a revered rock star virtually verbatim, like Pythia did the Oracle.

dunino *(n.)*
the torrent of crap, measured in column inches, that is unleashed when (a) an ageing rocker is left unguarded in a press conference and suggests he is more popular than God, or (b) a classical musician wears a slightly short skirt.

pickering nook *(n.)*
a setting used in publicity photos of young classical musicians in an attempt to make them seem approachable. Often involves some unique instrument positioning or, worse, a staged grouping around a dubious form of transport (golf buggies, miniature railways, etc.).

tushielaw *(n.)*
press photographers' rule, which states that if a female classical artist appears on the red carpet, she is

required to pose for at least one picture with her back to the camera, looking over her shoulder.

towie *(n.)*
a now-shelved 'classical music meets reality TV' project, originally planned for satellite TV, entitled *The Only Way is Einaudi*.

bonkle *(n.)*
a smiling, perma-tanned woman at an awards ceremony whose job it is to move the gongs from the table into the hands of the host.

swaffham bulbeck *(n.)*
a camera position beloved of TV concert directors in which the 'fish eye' reflection of a musician is seen in the shiny bell of a brass instrument, before panning out.

keelars tye *(n.)*
a tie that has suffered alcohol-induced adjustment during the latter part of an awards ceremony after the wearer realised that he was not going to win the category he was up for, and which is now cocked, high, tight and all skew-whiff, as is the wearer.

goonhusband *(n.)*

the amiable spouse of a particularly outspoken leading light of the arts educational world, who faithfully shows up several nights a week to a hugely diverse range of offerings and will speak at length about their life in systems analysis.

indian queens *(n.)*

collective noun for the type of *grandes dames* of any local cultural scene, who appear regularly in the town paper and maintain immaculate dowager hairstyles at all times. Usage example, overheard at Epping South Rotary Club Young Singer of the Year competition: ''Ere come the judges. And all the bigwigs. Look at that front row, reserved for the *Indian queens*. Anyone'd think it was *Mastersingers*!'

gignog *(n.)*

the drinks taken around on trays at posh musical launch parties. Usage example, overheard in Arts Council Christmas reception: 'Have you tried the miniature fish and chips? Bloody lovely – ooh, here's the chap with the *gignog*. Grab me a glass of whatever the yellow stuff is, will you? Make it two.'

keinton mandeville *(n.)*
a crucial manoeuvre at a musical launch party whereby one reaches behind oneself to steal a canapé or a
gignog (q.v.), from a passing waiter.

knaptoft *(n.)*
any drink taken at lunchtime by a musician who
knows they cannot drink at lunchtime.

clachan na luib *(n.; Celtic, archaic)*
the act of singing while intoxicated.

gerrick *(n.)*
any club for the artsy set that is so posh even its
members forget whereabouts along the street its dis-
creet front door is.

holnest *(n.)*
the pub with live music you stumble on one summer
on holiday, which subsequently becomes 'our place'
for two weeks.

howtel *(n.)*
the dive you can't believe you booked a night in purely because it was one minute from the music venue.

crew's hole *(n.)*
the pub closest to the stage door and therefore the most frequented.

densole *(adj.)*
descriptive of the sensible plimsolls worn by stage hands.

cathedine *(n.; slang)*
a single ear plug, chiefly used backstage.

ingatestone *(n.)*
the small black plastic keypads fixed alongside the doors to backstage areas, opened by the initiated with the aid of a mysterious access-all-areas fob.

corbets tey *(n.; slang)*
stage-hands' term for the base of a conductor's podium, prior to the brass rail being added. So named for the box that sat alongside the low chair used for the monologue in *The Two Ronnies*.

bagh a chaise *(n.)*
the classic 'podium, standard lamp and chair' combo, favoured by many establishments, as the stage

setting for the narrator/presenter in a children's work.

lickfold *(n.)*
an assistant who has been invited along as silent room meat for a pitch to a funding body for the next concert season.

king's pyon *(n.)*
singer's assistant whose chief role is to wait outside studios during interviews, playing Candy Crush.

gadlys *(n.)*
any brand of dark glasses worn indoors, usually by hipsters and crossover artists.

lopen head *(n.)*
the preferred haircut of rap stars, often involving the pattern of a Capability Brown maze razored onto the side of one's head.

vatersay *(adj.)*
descriptive of the speaking voice of either Willard White or Darth Vader.

llanwynell *(n.)*

spiel or patter used between songs by the man from the Go Compare advert.

innis chonain *(n.)*

early French nonsense minstrel, famous for his oft-set poem '*Comment dulcis, seyent idiot!*'

ealees *(n.)*

folk songs in which a blonde maiden is duplicitous. At the last count, 98 per cent of folk songs fall into this category.

dummer *(n.)*

early mime artist, term thought to have originated in Thaxted.

insh *(n.; pron. in-SHH)*

a state of silence in which only one's own internal soundtrack of bodily functions is audible.

eardiston *(n.)*

the most basic form of ear trumpet, formed by cupping the hand around one ear.

red post *(n.)*
a form of alexia or word blindness affecting the over-45s, rendering them unable to read a poster for a music event or distinguish the name of a band from that of a venue.

rickard's down *(n.)*
a musical insult masquerading as a compliment. An example, overheard in VIP area, Latitude: 'So that's your son's band . . . wow!' 'Yes, did you like them? He'll be so pleased you came!' 'Mmmm, they've got a real Darkness vibe about them . . .'

jenny lind *(adj.; slang)*
having been dumped by a loved one, i.e. binned (classic rhyming slang). Usage example, overheard in O2, prior to Andrea Bocelli concert: 'I don't believe it. She's just texted me to say she's not coming. I've been *jenny lind*.'

jaspar's green *(n.; slang)*
parents who are unaware of elements of pop culture, so named after the YouTube pair Joe and Caspar.

llanwynoro *(n.)*
the author's long-lost Welsh ancestors.

jingle street *(n.)*
a road in which a large number of residents opt to erect many, many outdoor Christmas lights, with some even resorting to the addition of piped festive music.

hobkirk *(n.)*
the person who has given out the hymn books on your way into church for more years than you can remember but whom you have never, ever seen outside the building.

winterborne muston *(n.)*
the smell given off from a cupboard full of *Hymns Old and New.*

church pulverbatch *(n.)*
the three cupboards of tattered old hymn books in the sacristy that haven't been used in forty years and now smell vaguely of walnuts.

pallaflat *(n.)*
a drawer unit built to hold sheet music, complete

with pull-down fronts that helpfully allow sheets to waft effortlessly to the floor.

tuckton *(n.)*
the central spine in a metronome, up and down which the *little weighton* (q.v.) slides to set the tempo. Many posit that the *tuckton* acquired its name from the satisfying 'tuc . . . tuc . . . tuc . . .' sound made by the action, as it swings to and fro.

little weighton *(n.)*
1. the small trapezoid disc of metal which is adjusted up and down the *tuckton* (q.v.) of a metronome to set the desired tempo.
2. *(slang)* musicians' term for a state of semi-arousal.

cringles *(n.)*
the small, circular plastic discs that fit in the centre of a 45 rpm record to make it playable on a turntable spindle.

clyro *(n.)*
a pen branded with the name of a British orchestra, given away free with a goodie bag at a conference.

hallsands *(n.)*
small buckets of sand, topped with cigarette butts and Nuttall's Mintoes wrappers, that one day may be called on to extinguish a fire the size of Basingstoke.

braes of yetts *(n.)*
shop in Haymarket, London, recognised as the finest maker of conductors' batons in the world, akin in reputation to Olivander's of Diagon Alley in the 'Harry Potter' books.

frome st quintin *(n.)*
near-legendary tea shop in Somerset where in 1964 Johnny Cash stopped for scones and ended up performing an acoustic set with local WI members; now marked with a black plaque.

fairlight cove *(n.)*
the rear section of a sheet-music shop where electrical equipment is sold; the line between the two is generally denoted by a cloud of patchouli oil.

high furze *(n.)*
as seen in old record shops and some hotel lifts, the phenomenon of the carpet not stopping at the end of

the floor but, for reasons unknown to anyone, continuing halfway up the wall.

cellardyke *(n.)*
the shadowy figure in the P.I.L. T-shirt who works in the basement of a vinyl store talking to as few customers as possible.

ACKNOWLEDGEMENTS

I would like to thank the lovely listeners to Classic FM's More Music Breakfast, without whom there would be no *Treasury*. Your constant inventiveness and ingenuity keeps me going every morning. You are a joy. Thanks to everyone who sent in place names, they are all much appreciated. I can't thank you each individually here, so instead I will single out Catherine Bott for her wonderful suggestion of Whitchurch Canonicorum.

Writing a book is a long and rewarding journey, involving many more people than just the author. I'm chiefly indebted to Olivia Bays at Elliott & Thompson for her nurturing support for this book, from the ideas stage to the very end of the publication process: I was chuffed to be able to include her own favourite place name in here, too. I remain ever grateful to Lorne Forsyth at Elliott & Thompson for his faith and support, and to the entire E&T team, particularly Pippa Crane, Alison Menzies, Jill Burrows and Lynn Hatzius, for their care, clarity and creativity.

I would also like to thank the wonderful people who work on Classic FM's More Music Breakfast, helping to foster the creative, positive and supportive environment, particularly our managing editor Sam Jackson, and Jenny Nelson and Phil Noyce. The team who are there with me every morning do a priceless job, including Will Kisby, my producer, music man Simon Funnell, and not forgetting Christy Evans. I am also grateful to the Classic FM presenter family, with a particular spotlight on John Suchet who is a great rock every morning, and Bill Overton whose professionalism and élan shines through each day. My thanks also to all the team at Classic FM, including our product manager, Caeshia St Paul, and our blast of sunshine senior publicity manager, John Chittenden – always a pleasure, John – and the extended Global family who make Classic FM such a vibrant place to work.

Finally, I would like to say a huge thank you to my family, Siobhan, Millie, Daisy and Finn, for being yumerous. Special thanks to Daisy, in fact, for her oft-repeated comment: 'You . . . are the living embodiment of humour!'

ABOUT CLASSIC FM

Classic FM is the UK's only 100 per cent classical music radio station, and the largest classical station in the world. Since it began broadcasting in September 1992, it has brought classical music to many millions of people. If you've yet to discover for yourself the delights of being able to listen to classical music twenty-four hours a day, you can find Classic FM on 101–102 FM, on Digital Radio, online at ClassicFM.com, on Sky channel 0106, on Virgin Media channel 922, on Freeview channel 731 and on FreeSat channel 721. You can also download the free Classic FM app, which will enable you to listen to Classic FM on your iPhone, iPod, iPad or Android device.

Classic FM has a long history of working to develop the next generation of classical music lovers, supporting organisations such as Music for Youth, which runs the annual Schools Prom at the Royal Albert Hall in London, and The Prince's Foundation for Children and the Arts, which has worked with the Philharmonia Orchestra to deliver an annual orchestral music education project to thousands of children across the UK, thanks to funding from the radio station's charity appeal.

Classic FM is owned by Global, the company behind the UK's three biggest commercial radio brands, Heart, Capital and Smooth, and the country's leading commercial talk station, LBC. Together, Global's brands reach 30 million people across the UK every week. Global also houses an entertainment division with expertise across talent management, publishing and live touring and festivals.

WORD FINDER